nërd girl

Rocks Paradise City

VISUAL & PERFORMING ARTS

nërd girl
Rocks Paradise City

A TRUE STORY
OF FAKING IT IN
HAIR METAL L.A.

Anne Thomas
Soffee

CHICAGO
REVIEW
PRESS

Library of Congress Cataloging-in-Publication Data

Soffee, Anne Thomas.

Nerd girl rocks paradise city : a true story of faking it in hair metal L.A./
    Anne Thomas Soffee.—1st ed.

       p. cm.

   ISBN 1-55652-586-9

   1. Soffee, Anne Thomas.

   2. Groupies—California—Los Angeles—Biography.

   3. Narcotic addicts—California—Los Angeles—Biography.

   4. Los Angeles (Calif.)—Biography.

   5. Richmond (Va.)—Biography. I. Title.

CT275.S5888A3 2005

979.4'94053'092—dc22   2005008628

Names, Real and Otherwise

Being a celebrity gets you a lot of perks, but it also means when you act up in public, people get to talk about it. Names of the famous and infamous have not been changed. As for my friends, associates, and partners in crime, I have generally changed names, physical characteristics, and identifying details unless they requested otherwise, and I thank those who requested otherwise for being good eggs. In making these changes I have tried to remain true to the spirit of What Actually Happened as much as I could.

Additionally, I am sure that hard-line Big Book thumpers are waiting to take me to task (again) for breaking the Eleventh Tradition and mentioning Alcoholics Anonymous by name instead of using the approved euphemism "a twelve-step program." This was an artistic choice that I did not make lightly. In short, everyone knows what "a twelve-step program" means, and in the end I chose to sacrifice anonymity in order to tell my story clearly and succinctly. If your recovery panties are all in a bunch about it, maybe you should talk to your sponsor about why you're so concerned about my anonymity.

Cover and interior design: Mel Kupfer
Cover image: © Erika Dufour/LuckyPix

Published by Chicago Review Press, Incorporated
814 North Franklin Street
Chicago, Illinois 60610
ISBN 1-55652-586-9
Printed in the United States of America
5   4   3   2   1

With love to my husband, Tad Hill,
who doesn't tease me (much) about my past

contents

acknowledgments

first and foremost, I offer humble thanks, apologies, and miss yous to all of my L.A. people: Marcia DePriest, David and Margaret Perry, Wayne Pemberton and Tye Smith, Andrew Lucchesi, Brian Frehner, Alex Almanza and the whole mediting crew, Triza Hogsett, Bud Thomas and everyone at the Blacklite, John Sykes, and Patrice Sena, to whom I owe more than I can say.

Between here and there, I tip my hat to Brigit Owers, Dave Schools, and Jim Morris, for putting me up and putting up with me.

Years later and miles away, I owe huge thanks to the people who have been super cool to me when I needed it most (and, in some cases, deserved it the least): Janiece Bernardini, Fran Tribble, Lucy Smith, Auntie Rocky, Karen Riddle, Melissa Burgess, Sabrina Starke, Vickie Holpe, Jeff Gordon, Lynn Barco, Betty and Raymond Millsaps, Randy Hallman, Tom DeHaven, Cynthia McMullen, John Chapin, Claudia Brookman, Sylvia Sichel, Tom Robbins, Mary Dyer Patillo, and Heather Short. Big thanks also to Bishop Walker, Doug Blanchard, Laura LaTour, Woodrow Hill, Kevin Musselman, Marilyn Flanagan, Stacey Ricks, and all the other cool people I met (and re-met) on book tour—you guys rock!

I couldn't get this done without such a bang-up crew. Seriously. I couldn't. I am completely beholden to Jane Dystel and everyone at Dystel and Goderich, and, at

Chicago Review Press, Cynthia Sherry, the indefatigable Catherine Bosin, Elizbeth Malzahn, and Sara Hoerdeman, and the coolest editor ever, Lisa Rosenthal, who actually takes the time to look up Stiv Bators because that's the kind of thorough gal she is.

And, finally, to my family, who continue to tolerate my public disclosures with grace and patience. George Soffee, Kevin and Christy Stone, Chuck and Mooty Jones, Mark Gershman, Herbert Gershman, Jason and Xine Soffee, Gary and Holly Bohannon, and, of course and always, extra big and grateful love to Ronnie and Dot Soffee. Apologies to my parents for writing another memoir. Don't forget, graduate school was your idea! Sincere and sheepish thanks to Rita and Jathan Stone, who I hope will overlook the scandalous content of this volume and instead focus on my excellent grammar and occasional literary references. In fact, you two should probably just stop reading here.

in memoriam

Hunter S. Thompson, Joey, Johnny, and Dee Dee Ramone,
Joe Strummer, Stiv Bators, Johnny Thunders, Elvis Presley,
and, of course, Lester Bangs

prologue

"That Girl Has a *Ring* in Her *Nose*"
Hipster Backlash and Metal Without Irony

FRESHMAN YEAR

"Could we please not listen to the Fuck You Music right now?" Maura, my long-suffering freshman roommate, begs for a reprieve from *Metallic KO* as she looks up from her desk full of calculus notes. Her assessment of my choice of music is right on; I got heckled by a bunch of frat boys again on my way back from the dining hall, and I am working out my aggression and disenfranchisement to Iggy and the Stooges, out of place as they may be here among the august halls of the College of William and Mary in colonial Williamsburg. I shrug my shoulders. I'm not deliberately trying to make life hard for Maura, but some things just call for Raw Power, and frat boys screaming "weirdo chick" is one of those things. If I'm stuck here at Chino Central, damn it, Iggy's coming with me, and there's nothing anybody can say to change that. Maura slams her book shut and storms down the hall to an Iggy-free zone, and I flop down on my single bed and stare up at my autographed Johnny Thunders poster and wonder how I'm going to last three and a half more years in this ivied pit.

Before I went to college, I never felt the need to wear my personality on my sleeve. Well, maybe *never* is too strong a word, but I left the fishnets and hair dye behind in middle school, along with most of the other outer trappings of my musical tastes. A Ramones T-shirt or a well-worn pair of combat boots said all I needed to say at Open High, my alternative public school; with mohawks and chains de rigueur in the student lounge, I stood out more by *not* standing out. Nobody yelled "weirdo" from the windows at my high school, like the boys in the dorm across the courtyard do when I walk out my door here at William and Mary. We may have been weird at Open High, but we were weird together, with our Friday night philosophy symposiums and existential literature classes that met in Monroe Park (street people welcome to join in any discussion). The closest we came to thinking *anyone* was weird was a raised eyebrow or two behind the back of Mark Russell, or, as we called him more often, "the Republican"— but even that rather sizeable quirk was accepted by the rest of us at Open in the spirit of diversity. The spirit of diversity is trumped by the spirit of '76 here, though—at William and Mary, the wrong logo on your polo shirt can make you a pariah and the slightest variation from convention is cause for public ridicule. I didn't know this when I agreed to come here.

Growing up near the Virginia Commonwealth University campus in Richmond, I thought college was a place for freethinkers and cool bands, girls with groovy retro go-go boots and guys in leather jackets. VCU is known for its art school. William and Mary is known for being really, really old. I should have realized things would be different there. Really different. And I would be miserable. Really miserable. Eventually, I give up. I'm obviously never going to fit

2

in, since everyone has already decided I'm a total freak based on what? My plain jean jacket and nonpastel sweaters? My simple blunt-cut bob and the tortoiseshell schoolboy frames I thought made me look so studious and collegiate? Tough crowd, these William and Mary folks, but I'm done playing to the crowd and I've got their weirdo right here. When the Fuck You Music stops working for me, I decide to show them what weirdo is all about. I have nothing to lose.

My first big step toward the reclaiming of my weirdness is the Piercing of the Nose. *Big deal,* I hear you say. *Just slide it under the door, won't you? Piercing is so planned community, so Hot Topic.* Allow me to remind you that this is Williamsburg, Virginia, in 1985. Nonstandard piercings have yet to hit the mainstream. Indeed, they won't even do them at the mall jewelry stores, and tattoo parlors won't be branching out into hole-punching for another few years. No, I'm on my own with this one, and with an ice cube, a needle, and *Give 'Em Enough Rope* cranked up really loud, I succeed in accessorizing my left nostril with an understated gold ring. Looking at my handiwork in the mirror, I am beyond pleased. The backdrop of my nerdy brown bangs and Mister Peabody glasses makes the nose ring look even weirder. Maura buries her face in her hands and shrieks. Just the effect I was going for. Perfect.

For two days, I am riding high. Walking across campus, I hear conversations stop in mid-sentence, disgusted sorority girl cries of "That girl has a *ring* in her *nose*!" Pity the weirdo kids of today, who can hang metal from their faces until they resemble a five-subject binder and never draw a second glance. It was so easy to shock at Williamsburg in 1985. Delighted with my success, I take to borrowing Maura's Laura Ashley dresses and matching headbands, just because the irony of the juxtaposition tickles me so. My British Literature professor forgets my name in the middle of asking me a question because he's so distracted by the nose ring. Maura refuses to eat lunch across the table from me in the dining hall, then proceeds to bring her sorority sisters over one by one to check it out. The cafeteria ladies ask questions and the football players curl their lips in disgust, which is no huge change from how they treated me before, but at least now I own it, because I chose the reason. I am weirdo, hear me roar!

My one concern is the same one that has plagued me since I first donned fishnets and leopard skin to sneak out to a punk show in seventh grade: the parents. Since I am conveniently an hour away in Williamsburg, my plan is to avoid coming home for the next four weekends to give my nostril time to heal. After that, I can slip the ring out just before I pull up in front of the house and no one will be the wiser or the more in trouble. That's the plan, anyway, until I spot my sister Christy crossing the student commons toward me a week into my great adventure. Two years ahead of me and obedient to a fault, her presence is a constant reminder that my parents are only fifty miles and a collect call away—a call she never hesitates to make when she feels like I am "ruining her good name," which is frequently. Known as "the Bod" on Fraternity Row, my sister is the universal object of unrequited lust, shaped like a centerfold and staunchly and unremittingly Catholic to the

4

core. In a particularly galling example of ironic justice, she ends up ruining *my* good name when one particularly loathsome Phi Tau pads his resume by claiming he's bedded "one of the Soffee girls." Thanks to my sister's legendary chastity, everyone assumes it's me—besides, you know how those weirdo chicks like the freaky stuff. Still, I dutifully allow her to drag me along to keg parties and mixers, where she introduces me to leering football players and oxford-clad cads who shake my hand while staring down the front of her blouse.

I hope against hope that maybe she doesn't see me, but no, she's waving. Maybe she's late for class and will just keep on walking! No such luck there, either. She's headed straight for me. With a sense of impending doom, I lift my intro psychology text higher, higher, until it covers everything below my eyes. Then I peer out from behind it, trying my best to act nonchalant.

"Hey." My voice is muffled by 300 pages of *Freud und Jung*. "What's going on?"

She's not buying it. Her eyes narrow, the same way they do when I make my command appearances by her side at frat parties wearing baggy jeans and slouchy black sweaters. It doesn't take much on my part to set off her Ruining-My-Good-Name Meter, and I know this is going to blow it right off the scale, surpassing even the time she sent me home to change into "something dressier" for a Kappa Sig mixer and I came back wearing a vintage off-the-shoulder cocktail dress, seamed fishnets, and my only new clothing purchase since starting college—a pair of brand-spanking-new, first-run Air Jordan basketball shoes. You know, for all the hoops

I shoot. I think she actually cried that night.

Q: *Do you really shoot hoops?*

A: *Sorry. It was a poor attempt at humor, since you can't see that I am every bit of five-foot-two. Not that height has anything to do with it. I made the mistake of asking one of my European History study-group partners if he played basketball, since he was well over six feet tall. He scowled and asked me if I played miniature golf. So much for making friends with casual banter.*

"What's your problem?" She makes a grab for the book, but I hang on for dear life.

"Nothing! Just, you know, studying." I make a quick switch, dropping the book at the same time as I raise a sweatshirt-covered hand and place it oh-so-casually along-side of my nose. You know, like Santa Claus, if Santa Claus was about to get bitch-slapped by his older sister for wearing a nose ring.

"Ohhhhhhh . . ." Her eyes narrow even more as she grabs the cuff of my sweatshirt. "You *didn't!*" and with one good yank she pulls my arm away, revealing my forbidden adornment. I suck in my breath, waiting for what I know is coming. The one ace my sister knows she always has, and has never once hesitated to use. She sneers disgustedly at me and hikes her backpack up on her shoulder before delivering the standard line.

"*I . . . am . . . telling.*"

"So tell," I say with mock-bravado. She knows and I know that she's beaten me, but I have my pride. "I don't

care. I'll tell them first! I'll call them tonight!" Yeah. Right.
No matter, because she's already stalked off across Barks-
dale Field, flipping her hair at me, in a hurry to get away
before anyone sees her talking to me. You know, good
name and all that. I sigh into my psychology textbook, realizing that my days as a cutting-edge style-maker are numbered. I pack up my books and head out to stroll through
the tourist area one more time before I have to go back to
being the plain old weirdo chick I was a week ago. It's
times like this I understand why my dad was so hot for me
to go to William and Mary. He already had a narc waiting.

That night, I break my usual self-imposed social exile
to accompany my friend Stacey to a party hosted by the
college radio station. Stacey is doing her freshman purga-
tory as a radio station grunt in the hope that she'll be
granted one of the crappier time slots for her own radio
show when she becomes a sophomore. My own music nerd
arrogance prevented me from doing the same; having
already hosted a show for two years on cable radio in Richmond, I told the WCWM station manager that I'd be
damned if I was going to file records at a *college* station,
thank you—which basically means I shot myself in the foot
with the one group of William and Mary students with
whom I might have gotten along.

Q: *So you earned your rock 'n' roll cred working at a cable radio
station?*

A: *Actually, the radio station was a side gig, even though my
show was really cool—I did an hour and a half of sixties garage*

*rock and an hour and a half of seventies New York punk. I just
kind of slid into the radio gig through my writing internship at a
local independent monthly paper called* ThroTTle. *It was billed
as "The Magazine of Acceleration for the Eighties" (ahem), and it
accelerated me from writing op-ed pieces for the photocopied
Open High School newspaper to interviewing Henry Rollins and
cadging free passes to hardcore shows before I could even drink.
Well, legally, anyway.*

The radio station folks are the closest thing William and
Mary has to a music scene, which is sad because I can't
stand any of the music they play on the station. It's all spectacles and shaggy hair and thrift-store paisley shirts, Throwing Muses and They Might Be Giants and Camper Van
Beethoven. The bands have clever names and cleverer lyrics
and wouldn't know a power chord if it bit them on the ass.
These bands are rock 'n' roll like Kenny G is jazz. It's all
too clean and smart for me. But I need to parade my nose
ring around one last time before I am forced to take it out,
and a radio station party is as good a place as any, so I dutifully trot out a Misfits T-shirt and a pair of holey jeans and
make the long hike over to the off-campus party to wow
the plebeians with my unbelievable punk rockitude.

"Hey, cutie," Stacey says when I sneak up behind her at
the party. A big girl, Stacey favors drapy ankle-length layers
in various shades of moss and stone. Tonight, she's also
wearing a porkpie hat and a jean jacket with a Let's Active
album cover painted on the back. Her randomly assigned
freshman roommate, Emily, is a pocket-sized butch lesbian
with a mohawk. They are the wacky friends in the sitcom

that is my freshman year. Stacey passes me a beer and I look around the party. It is a sea of Bono haircuts and Lennon glasses across both sexes. I think of what I am missing at home, and I sigh. For this I gave up punk rock matinees and coffeehouses. Aside from Stacey and Emily, I have no friends at William and Mary. Aside from the universally unappealing pencil-necked weird-guy suitors who think I'll date them just because I'm weird too, I have no social life. And, aside from weekends and summers, I have no reprieve. This is what I have to look forward to for the next three and a half years of my life. I open my throat and pour down the rest of my bottle joylessly. Hooray for the best years of my life.

"Nice nose ring." I look up and see Jack Pettinger, the premed junior who hosts the Friday night trivia show on the radio station. Short and stocky, with a shock of curly blond hair, he looks like he belongs in a striped shirt with a slingshot in his back pocket, not at the alma mater of presidents. He's grinning like an idiot and nodding at his suave opening line. *Another loser who thinks he's in my league, the poor fool.* I nod back warily, waiting for the wooing to begin.

"Thanks." I look around for quick access to another beer, and while I am looking away, he unbuttons his shirt. I am silently wondering *what the fuck* when I see the reason. Jack Pettinger, radio station trivia geek and yellow-haired kid, is wearing 10-gauge BDSM rings in both nipples. Where I was the punk rockingest kid on campus five minutes ago, I am now a wannabe piker. Satisfied with my dumbfounded expression, Jack buttons his purple paisley shirt back up and struts away, way too undercover cool to waste his time talking to a wannabe piker like me.

JUNIOR YEAR

"What is this *crap* you're listening to?" Stacey plops herself down on the couch and squints at the television, where a spandexed blonde writhes underneath a wailing guitar.

"Bite your tongue—that's *Lita Ford,*" I say reverently, then quickly realize that Stacey might not even know who Lita Ford is—or, more important, was. "You know, Lita Ford from the Runaways? Joan Jett, Jackie Blue? *Cherie Currie?*" Even my rock-hating sister could pick Cherie Currie out of a lineup, if only because she played opposite Scott Baio in the bad-girl drama *Foxes,* a Jodie Foster Cinemax classic rife with hotdogging skateboard scenes, a plethora of tube tops, and even an Angel concert at no added cost. Stacey blinks at me, shrugs, and lights a cigarette. College radio people don't know from seventies glam rock. "Kim Fowley," I howl, as if this will trigger some recognition. "CHERRY BOMB!"

Nothing. To Stacey, this is just cheesy heavy metal she's seeing on MTV, made that much cheesier by virtue of being played by a scantily clad bimbo. I know that's no bimbo, though—that's *Saint Lita* of the Runaways, Lita who sits at the right hand of Suzi Quatro in the hierarchy of all that is holy to rocker chicks. But Stacey doesn't know. Doesn't care, either, and gets up and heads to the kitchen to cadge a soda. I am duty bound to stay and watch, because the Runaways represent all that is rock 'n' roll to me, the same way that Iggy Pop and Ziggy Stardust and Sid Vicious do. The Runaways were dirty and mean and a little bit greasy, with their feathered hair and too-thick blue eyeshadow. They wore Lip Smackers and satin jackets and Candie's slides, everything I remember about the seventies, only that much more, because they were teenagers on the Sunset Strip and I was just a chubby little third-grader in Richmond, Virginia. Even then, though, I knew. In my third-grade class picture, you can see that I knew. I was the one in the Alice Cooper T-shirt.

This is the whole problem with me and the college radio people. They don't want their music greasy and dumb like I do. They want clever couplets and wordplay from English majors and poets wearing clean shirts. They want music you have to think about and lyrics that make you rifle through the files in your prep school head until you go "ah, yes, they're referencing Joyce!" I don't ever want to go "ah, yes," and I certainly don't want to do it when I'm listening to rock 'n' roll. I want to bite my bottom lip and maybe flip somebody off. I want to stop just short of playing air guitar and cuss a lot. I want to feel like maybe if I ran into the Runaways behind the 7-Eleven, they would let me hang out with them. I don't want to feel like I'm in school. I'm already in school enough. And I'm not going to tell Stacey, but even if Lita Ford hadn't been a Runaway, I kinda like this song. I mean, what's not to like about a tough chick who sings about getting laid and fighting in a bar?

Q: *So I take it you weren't an REM fan.*

A: *Funny, that. I saw REM open for Gang of Four at the Empire Theater when I was in ninth grade. Maybe it was an off night, but they pretty much blew their chance with me then and there. Anemic is the word that comes to mind, and about the only word, which tells you how much of an impression they did not make on me. I could never really get it up for them after that, even though all the paisley-clad music journalist types at* ThroTTle *loved them. Give me Stiv Bators over Michael Stipe any day.*

Stacey comes back from the kitchen with a Coke for me and reclaims her spot on the couch. Reaching across the coffee table, she picks up a magazine. Not just any magazine. The magazine that has single-handedly restored my faith in music journalism and maybe music itself. The magazine that made me fail my British Poetry exam last week, so enraptured was I with my new find. Not since I was in eighth grade, poring over the latest issue of *CREEM*, devouring articles on Iggy and Blondie and the New York Dolls have I found a magazine that speaks to my soul like this one does. I am in love.

"*Ick,*" Stacey says, and drops the magazine back on to the coffee table.

"What do you mean, *ick?* That magazine is *fantastic,*" I say, picking it up. I had stumbled across it completely by accident the previous Monday night. In the throes of yet another night-before-the-test all-nighter, I developed a pressing need for more caffeine—real caffeine, not soda or chocolate. Late-night bottom-of-the-pot Tinee Giant caffeine. I made the trek across campus at three A.M.

Dark and deserted, the early morning hours were the

only time I truly liked William and Mary. The bright green
Olde English letters on the roof of the Tinee Giant were
like a beacon, calling to me, singing a song of something
seedy and base that I had been craving more than I'd been
craving coffee. Propped on the metal news rack between
People and *Rolling Stone* was a magazine I'd never seen
before—*Rip*.

"ATTENTION MOSHERS, BANGERS, THRASHERS,
HESHERS, SLAMMERS, AND ROCKERS! IT'S ALL
HERE!" blared the purple cover. I was intrigued—and only
partly because I didn't know what a hesher was. I picked up
the magazine and leafed through it. I saw bands I recognized from the punk rock days—Agnostic Front, Mötor-
head, Suicidal Tendencies—and a lot of screeching guitars
and greasy-looking singers, but what really intrigued me
was the cover. Two guys who looked like the second coming of T-Rex—one skinny, sneering, and wearing a snake-
skin jacket, his lank hillbilly-red hair falling from a leather
cap, the other snarling and unshaven, with a stovepipe hat
perched above a mop of curls à la Noddy Holder. These
were my people, the kind of greasy, gutter-dwelling punks
and lowlifes I'd idolized since I read my first *CREEM* magazine in sixth grade. These were my heroes, my muses, in all
of their stringy-haired glory. They were what was missing
from college radio—rawness, stupidity, and filth. They
tugged at something deep inside of me, something left over
from afternoons spent listening to Patti Smith and Johnny
Thunders. This was what I had been looking for. This was
where I belonged. This was where I wanted to be. I bought
the magazine and read it over and over, instead of John

Donne and Andrew Marvell and Percy Bysshe Shelley, who probably wouldn't have minded. The men don't know, but the little girls understand.

Q: *Let me get this straight. You were so impressed with a* magazine *that you stayed up all night, reading it repeatedly and thereby failing your final exam?*

A: *I wasn't impressed, I was obsessed. If you were born without the gene for obsession, thank your lucky stars right now. You will never lie awake nights wondering how you are going to get tickets to a sold-out concert in Canada and get there and get back when you've only got $125 to your name. You are spared the endless search for a 12" copy of "Miss You" on pink vinyl with a picture sleeve, backed with "Far Away Eyes." You will never have to explain to the policeman who pulled you over for weaving that you were merely looking for a music store that might still be open at 11:30 at night because you just realized that the bass riff of the Who's "Substitute" is a direct steal from "Nineteenth Nervous Breakdown" and you've absolutely got to find it right now so you can listen and compare.*

However, you will also never know the joy of rooting through three boxes of LPs on someone's dew-covered front lawn and finally unearthing the holy frail, an actual 3D cover mono copy of Their Satanic Majesties Request. *You won't hand it to the homeowner and wait breathlessly silent, hoping he won't realize the value of what he has, then chew your lip as you give him the twenty-five cents he asks for so you won't blurt out the truth before you get away with your prize. (And, before you judge me, remember we didn't have eBay back then. Thank God.)*

"Those guys on the cover are from Guns N' Roses," I say, making a futile stab at relaying their coolness in words. "Hang out for a little while and maybe the video will come on. The guy on the right does this snake dance thing, and he's got on purple eye-shadow and his voice is all screechy."

"And that's supposed to make me want to stay why, exactly?"

"No, it's really cool! And he goes *'you know where you are? You're in the jungle, baby! You're gonna die!'* It's cool."

"Yeah, you said that already," Stacey says, leafing half-heartedly through the magazine. "Hey, look. These girls don't shave under their arms! Is that the new style? Does that mean I can stop shaving under mine? Because that would really save me some hassle."

"Those aren't girls. That's Poison. But really. And the guitar player from Guns N' Roses looks like 1972 Keith Richards and he has a nose ring."

"Well, that I might stay for." Stacey and I have cake and Jack Daniels for Keith Richards's birthday every year. He hasn't shown up yet, but we're still hoping. "Can we at least mute it?"

"We'd better not. I had it muted while I was on the phone yesterday, and I thought I was watching a Bon Jovi video and it turned out to be Stevie Nicks. It was kind of traumatic." Stacey nods sympathetically. We may not be on the same page with Guns N' Roses, but nobody wants to be caught ogling Stevie Nicks. *Leather and Lace* notwithstanding, she ain't no Lita Ford.

"Hey," Stacey says, changing the subject somewhat obviously. "Do you want to go to Norfolk this weekend to see the Waxing Poetics?" See what I mean about the clever names? I shake my head, not sorry at all to be missing out on that fun.

"I'm going home this weekend. I've got stuff to do." What I'm not letting on is that the stuff I have to do consists of drinking domestic beer and watching *Headbanger's Ball* with a bunch of rivethead friends I made over Christmas break—forklift drivers and drywallers, guys with mullets and concert T's who don't see the irony in any of this, not even in Judas Priest's high-camp leather daddy shtick. They have an unnamed band that plays dead-on covers of Blue Öyster Cult and Sabbath in a wood-paneled basement behind Lakeside Baptist Church, and I cram on the ratty plaid couch between the drummer's girlfriend and the singer's roommate and sing along. It's a dirty little secret that is easily covered by my general dislike of the social scene at William and Mary. I'm usually not around on the weekends anyway, so nobody suspects that I'm a closet metalhead of the nonironic kind.

It isn't that the college radio people mind me listening to Poison and Bon Jovi. They don't mind that I show up to their parties in leather pants and an Iron Maiden T-shirt with the sleeves hacked off. This is all cute to them in a *hey-guys-let's-go-to-the-truckstop-at-midnight* kind of way, the same way Elvis busts and pink flamingos are cute to them. As long as they think I have my tongue firmly in my cheek the whole time I am rocking out, I suffer no hipster backlash. But what they don't know is I am dead serious. When I crank up the new Faster Pussycat album, my heart is in every note. I don those leather pants with utmost seriousness, just as Lita Ford and Suzi Quatro donned them before me. They'll never understand that, and I've resigned myself to having to hide it Monday through Friday. Since Christmas, though, I've gone home every weekend to watch *Headbanger's Ball* in the basement with my new buds, none of whom expect me to snicker up my sleeve at Nikki Sixx's hairpiece, and none of whom ever mention James Joyce or Michael Stipe.

Which is absolutely jake with me.

1

"I'm Left, You're Right, She's Gone"
King-Sized Beds and the King Himself on the Road to L.A.

Since I was in middle school, I dreamed of becoming the next Lester Bangs. Just in case you weren't greedily devouring music rags like I was in the 1970s, Lester wrote for everything I read as a teenager— *CREEM, New York Rocker, Rolling Stone*, you name it. He was gonzo and edgy and passionate about the music and the words he used to describe it. As close as you could get to being a rock star while still being an English nerd—as in the subject, not the nationality—Lester was just as likely to turn up in the gossip columns as he was in a byline. I hung on his every word, and when he died in 1982, I felt destined to pick up the mantle, as I'm sure plenty of other little punk rock nerds like myself did all across the country. I got a jump on the other would-be Bangses by getting my foot in the door at *ThroTTle*, where they published me far more often and with far fewer edits than they probably should have, subjecting Richmond readers to my teenage would-be gonzo musings on everything from MTV to Chick Tracts to *Soldier of Fortune* magazine. So when I graduate from William and Mary I already have a sizeable portfolio of press clips, some pretty damn good and some cringeworthy, but each bearing my name in smudgy black ink on the byline, which is what matters in the end, right?

Clips in hand, I immediately begin searching for my jumping-off point to music journalism greatness, mailing my resume and portfolio to every single rag on the newsstand that sports a bare-chested guitarist on its cover.

Q: *Lester Bangs. Lester Bangs. The name sounds familiar, but not being a punk rock nerd, I can't really place it.*

A: *I'll bet I know why. While checking some facts for this book, I was heartened—and actually a little misty—to note the number of teenagers and twentysomethings in the online communities who list "Lester Bangs" among their generally less cool interests. I was misty and heartened, that is, until I checked further into their little blogworlds and found that it wasn't the real Lester Bangs they admired, but the fictionalized portrayal of him—by a suave, unpudgy actor—in the movie* Almost Famous. *You know, kinda like all those kids who like "Lust for Life" because they heard it on the* Trainspotting *soundtrack. Only more horrible.*

Even though my dream of being the next Lester Bangs is alive, the rock journalism industry is terminal, bordering on critical. Some of the magazines to which I'm applying are so poorly written I am almost ashamed to be seen buying them. "Vince Neil met his wife Sharise at the club she was a mud wrestler at," one caption in *Metal Edge* blathers, its preposition sticking out almost as far as Sharise's muddy tits. It makes me wistful for afternoons spent in my bedroom, poring—or "pouring," as *Metal Edge* would say— over the latest issue of *CREEM*. Not just a music magazine, *CREEM* was challenging reading, stuff that made you think.

Even the letters to the editor (mine numbered three, thanks) were filled with clever asides and obscure musical references that made you fairly tingle just by knowing you were one of the select few who caught them. You were as likely to find Miles Davis as Van Halen in Robert Christgau's record reviews, and irony was the order of the day. *CREEM* stopped publishing in 1988, leaving me high and dry when I finished college the next year. Ladies and gentlemen, Boy Howdy has left the building.

Naturally, when one's dreams are dashed by the newsprint gods, the only logical rejoinder is to gift wrap a ham. Allow me to clarify. At this point I have finished college, I have no plans for my future, no destiny to fulfill, and no money in my pocket. Figuring I can address two out of these three with a pick-up job while I ponder the third, I take a stylin' gig at the mall making gourmet Virginia gift baskets for people with a lot of money and a desire for more salt in their diet (a *lot* more salt—consider that the two main ingredients in the top-selling basket are Virginia Diner peanuts and Smithfield Ham). Living on sample peanuts and food-court lunches, I spend my spare time sending clips and queries to music magazines and drinking beer at Newgate Prison, Richmond's only metal bar— and the less said about it, the better. All of this excitement follows the year's main event, which was me following the East Coast leg of the Rolling Stones' *Steel Wheels* tour in a perfectly adorable used Hyundai my dad gave me as a graduation gift. I have a feeling if he'd known what was coming, he would have considered a nice savings bond or something.

Q: *Did the Stones tour come as a result of some great journalistic opportunity? Was this not the assignment of a lifetime?*

A: *No, it was not. It was the culmination of a decade of fandom bordering on sick obsession. Not that I didn't try to get some kind of sponsorship, press credentials, something, anything—but come on. These are the Stones. Even magazines like* Rolling Stone *itself reserve that assignment for the big names and celebrity guest writers, the Dave Marshes and Stanley Booths, not peons like me with a few local bylines and a deep and abiding love for side one of* Exile on Main Street. *But yeah, I came, I saw, I sang along. It fucking* rocked.

As if it isn't demeaning enough to be a shop girl instead of a jet-setting rock journalist, I have to swallow the bitter pill that is the fact that my William and Mary nemesis, the director of the college radio station, is now writing for *Rolling Stone*. Even though I know that she had to pay her dues at Wenner-owned *US* magazine before cracking the RS nut, just seeing her byline rubs three hams' worth of salt into my *Rolling Stone*-byline-less wounds—and it stings. Honestly, I don't even like *Rolling Stone*; it's too mainstream and dry for my journalistic taste, and probably sour to boot. My resume has been sent to the smaller, more creative rags, like *Alternative Press, Spin*, and, of course, *Rip*. And I haven't gotten so much as a form letter back from any of them. Eventually I grow desperate and start sending resumes to every music magazine on the stands (except *Rolling Stone*, of course, not that I'm bitter).

I lower my goals, informing *Metal Maniacs* that I counted no less than twenty-seven spelling and grammatical errors in their latest issue and, for a small fee, I'd be glad to make myself available for copy editing. Go figure why they didn't hire me right away.

And so it goes, letter after letter, beer after beer, and gift-wrapped ham after gift-wrapped ham, until the fateful day arrives when I finally receive a hand-addressed letter from the imaginatively titled *Metal* magazine. I tear it open, hoping to see the typewritten equivalent of hosannas and heavenly choirs—*here she is to save rock journalism, come on out, your corner office is waiting.* Instead, I'm greeted not with the usual form letter, but with a personal note from editor Steve Peters relaying the noncommittal but not entirely discouraging news that *Metal* works mainly with freelance writers and I'm free to stop by their Hollywood office if I'm ever in the area and see about open assignments.

Well, a nod's as good as a wink to a blind bat, and a maybe's as good as a yes to a ham-wrapping would-be rock writer. Before my parents have even had a chance to recover from the Rolling Stones tour, I'm loading up the car to make my fortune as a freelance heavy metal journalist in Los Angeles. It's been almost a year since I finished college, and all I have to show for it is a folder full of tearsheets from the same free local weeklies I was writing for when I was in high school. If I'm planning to follow in Lester Bangs's footsteps, I only have a decade to get famous before my untimely death from mixing cold medicine with Darvon, so I'd better get cracking. Nobody ever hit it big reviewing Holiday Inn lounge bands in Richmond, Virginia.

Q: *Didn't Pat Benatar get her start singing for a Holiday Inn lounge band in Richmond?*

A: *Yes. Remember all of those great reviews she got that catapulted those writers to journalistic stardom? Neither do I.*

Inasmuch as one can "plan" a move to a city three thousand miles away where one has no friends, no job, and nowhere to live, I start planning the move. By this I mean I map out the route that will take me past the greatest number of my faraway friends, friends who understand why this is a perfectly sensible plan, that will allow me to visit the most cool places, and, naturally, the route that takes me past Graceland, because what rock 'n' roll pilgrimage would be complete without a trip to Graceland? In a well-worn Rand McNally atlas that already bears the thick neon-green paths I followed on the Rolling Stones tour, I map my desired stops—Graceland and Sun Records, then down to the Blues Archive in Oxford, Mississippi, and William Faulkner's grave right down the street (I may have a rock 'n' roll heart, but my brain is pure English major), across the bottom of the country to New Mexico and Arizona, two states where I've got buds who will put me up and put up with me, and then on to Los Angeles. Much to the shock of my rivethead friends, I plan to make the first stop on my pilgrimage in Athens, Georgia, of all places. Athens, home of REM, Pylon, and enough paisley shirts and pegged pants to fill every overpriced thrift store in Georgia, represents everything I hate about music and, more important, music journalism. Rock journalists like Athens bands because Athens bands are basically rock critics with guitars. Nerds and outcasts with too many albums. I should know, I am one. But I also know that I would make a really lame rock star. Apparently no one told Michael Stipe.

I'm going to Athens to bury REM, not to praise them. I'm planning to visit three of my old Deadhead buddies who moved to Athens for college and never left. Chris got a job working for Coca-Cola, James is moving toward a career in political lobbying, and Dave, though none of us know it yet, is changing the face of the Athens music scene playing bass in his new band, Widespread Panic. Everyone's been humoring Dave for the past few years, figuring he'll outgrow this long-haired hippie phase and get a real job, but not me. I know what it is to want to spend the rest of your life on this stuff because nothing else makes you feel like yourself. I'll say it again—the men don't know, but the little girls understand. Even though Widespread Panic's meandering jams have little to do with loud, fast rules, Dave is following his musical muse and that makes me more than happy. For Dave and the guys, I will tolerate much paisley. I plan to stay in Athens for a week.

Q: *OK, hold the phone. You were a Deadhead?*

A: *Although I do have dancing skeletons in my closet, it would be more accurate to say that I went through a period in which I ran with Deadheads, and availed myself of their, uh, generosity. In short, when I was in high school, I had older friends with IDs and connections who were Deadheads, and so, yes, I did travel to some Dead shows, and I did do some noodle dancing, although I* *did so in an Agnostic Front T-shirt. Patchouli was worn. Mistakes were made. You would be fair to think less of me for this.*

To my surprise, my plans are not met with the celebration and rah-rah knock 'em dead spirit I expected from my friends. There is a lot of grumbling from my metalhead buddies about upcoming shows I'll miss, never mind the plethora of shows I'll be able to see on any given day in Los Angeles. My old Deadhead buds humor my hair-metal fetish as a crazy phase I'm going through and seem almost worried that I'm serious enough about it to relocate. The only one of my friends who is behind my plans is Stacey, who can't wait for updates on my upcoming brushes with cheesy greatness in the form of all of the hair gods and has-beens who populate the Sunset Strip. We have our own double feature movie night, *Foxes* and *Decline of Western Civilization Part II: The Metal Years*. I can't decide who I want to be more, Lita Ford or Cherie Currie. Stacey is just happy that Poison is in *Decline*, and she cheers when C. C. DeVille says if he weren't a rock star, he'd be a shoe salesman. Stacey is inordinately amused by Poison.

Pity my poor parents, who pepper me with foolish questions like *where are you going to stay when you get to L.A.?* and *what if you don't get enough work to make a living?* I know it is the job of parents to be sensible, but *maaaaaaaan*, what a buzzkill. I am resolute in the face of reason and logic. I am moving to Los Angeles and that's all they need to know. My father's steadfast sense of denial works in my favor; after about half a dozen "why-in-the-shit" questions go unanswered, he clicks over into pretending I'll change my

mind and leaves me alone. My mother is a bit more prob-
lematic, demanding TripTiks, bank statements, and backup
plans. I'm not sure why she's even bothering; we've already
seen this movie anyway, and we know how it ends. Just like
the year that I traded the colonial confines of William and
Mary for Bejing Linguistics Institute, just for a change of
scene, they know I'm prone to rash decisions and hastily
packed suitcases, and that nothing they say or do will
change my mind when I decide there's somewhere else I
need to be. They know that I'm going and I know that
they'll pretend I'm not until the day I leave. I put in my
notice at the mall and prepare to hit the highway.

Q: *Beijing? As in Beijing, China?*

A: *It sure wasn't Kansas, Dorothy. Yeah, weirdo that I was, I took
Chinese for my foreign language requirement, and one thing led
to another, and well, Beijing. That's a whole 'nother story and
not a particularly rocking one, but I will share with you one
glimpse of my efforts to bring Lou Reed to the masses of the People's Republic. I call it* Scene from a Taxicab, *and it has been
translated from the Mandarin by yours truly.*

Me: *Could you play this while you drive, please? Thanks.
(I hand the cabdriver a Velvet Underground cassette to replace the
European synth-pop mix that all cabdrivers in Beijing have been
issued.)*

Radio: *Opening strains of "Sister Ray," Lou Reed moaning
about hitting his mainline over screeching guitar feedback.*

Irritated Chinese Cabdriver (ICC): *Is this what people listen to in America?*

Me: *Yes, it is.*

ICC: *No, what I mean is, do a lot of people in America listen to this, or do just you and a few other people listen to this?*

Me (grumbling): *Well . . . me and a few other people.*

ICC: *Aha! That's what I thought. How about One Glove Black Man? Everybody likes him, right?*

Just like when I left for Beijing, and when I left for the Rolling Stones tour, my impending departure is ignored until the eve of the very day that I leave, and then I am suddenly a horrible, horrible daughter, causing heartbreak and anxiety, and I eat dinner by myself, because everyone has locked themselves in their room so as not to see my soon-to-be-leaving face. I season my lonely meal with tears of remorse and guilt, guilt that I know I deserve every gut-wrenching bit of, but that I also know I must bear without crumbling, because the only way that I could ever possibly please my parents would be if I live in my childhood room until I'm fifty and spend every waking hour eating and appreciating their food, and I'm sorry, but this ain't that kind of party.

Q: *Surely you don't mean your parents would really have you cloistered for life if they had their way.*

A: *Listen. The ass-kicker is, something like buying a can of peas when he thinks I should buy green beans upsets my dad just as much as me taking off on some half-cocked globe-trotting adventure. So I've learned that sometimes you've just gotta buy the peas and pay the piper. I love my dad with all my heart, but sometimes you need a can of peas.*

So after a festive solitary farewell dinner of Fruity Pebbles, I spend my final night in my bed at my parents' house and roll out the next morning to head for Athens completely without fanfare—true to form, my parents have gotten up extra-early for work so they wouldn't have to see me leave. Unfortunately, the most haphazardly laid plans are almost guaranteed to go awry, it seems, and Dave is on tour in California of all places when I finally roll into Athens in mid-August. I'm sorry not to see him, but on the upside it leaves me quartered in high style in the "rock star suite," as Chris and James jokingly call Dave's room. Small, shabby, and humid, just like their rooms, Dave's bedroom is set apart only by the presence of a giant waterbed, purchased with real rock star dollars! Never mind the crumpled copies of *Relix* and dirty socks that Dave has left in his wake—this is still big luxury. I stretch out on the bed my first night in Athens, my toes not even beginning to reach the end of the mattress, and sway back and forth with the motion of the water. I know that it is not the lot of the rock 'n' roll journalist to ever see even a fraction of the money that a musician sees, but I feel hopeful that maybe a king-sized waterbed is somewhere in my future. In an interview with *CREEM* in 1981, Rick James told Dave

DiMartino that his goal was to make "Paul McCartney White Boy Money." I may not be able to aspire to that as a gonzo journalist, but I think that Dave Schools Rock Star Money may be within my grasp. Visions of waterbeds and bylines dance in my head as I drift off to sleep.

It turns out that I have sold Athens short, as I have with most things I've condemned prior to investigation. There is an overabundance of paisley, to be sure, and homages to fortunate sons REM are around every corner, from clubs that they own a stake in, to restaurants that tout them as regulars, but so are quirky used record stores, dusty old rummage shops, and diners that offer huge plates of biscuits and gravy at three in the morning for under five bucks. The lazy gentility makes Athens feel like it's back in time, and the cost of living is rock-bottom compared even to Richmond. I see now why the guys never came back after college, and it makes me even more apprehensive about my destination. From what I know of Los Angeles, the prices are high, the people are phony, and everything is slick, plastic, and devoid of character. I know there won't be biscuits and gravy served up with sweet tea by waitresses who call me baby, and if there were I probably wouldn't be able to afford them because they'd be considered some kind of kitschy Beverly Hills delicacy. The guys sense my apprehension and waste no time trying to talk me out of proceeding with my plans and call it foreshadowing when a homeless man at the Varsity Diner treats us to an out-of-the-blue rant about a new restaurant in town that charges two dollars for a cup of coffee.

"I didn't pay it! No sir, I didn't! Do you know what I

told them? I said, well, maybe nobody told you when you came up the road, no I don't think they did, but I'm here to tell you, you in *Georgia* now, boy, and you can't charge those L.A. prices! You hear what I told him? You can't charge those L.A. prices! That's the kinda price they charge in L.A., not Georgia, no sir!" For the rest of the week James and Chris repeatedly remind me of "L.A. prices," as if I might not already realize that I am biting off more than I can chew. By the time I head out of Athens bound for Graceland, I am filled with self-doubt: *What if I can't find anywhere I can afford to live? What if I don't get enough assignments to pay my rent? What if I get on the L.A. freeway and can never get off, like Charley on the MTA?* It may be a Kingston Trio song, but it instills the kind of fear that only Elvis can cure, and I know that I need to leave Athens and make my way to Graceland posthaste, before I have time to change my mind.

I know in my heart that Graceland will set me straight, but I'm still three states away, so I have to fend off the urge to turn the car around with as much rock 'n' roll as I can muster. I play Lynyrd Skynyrd tapes all the way through Alabama, singing along with "Freebird" at the top of my lungs like a good southern girl. (Hey, it's not my usual gig, but when in Rome and all that.) I can tolerate some southern-fried boogie right now, because my next stop will be Mississippi, birthplace of the blues, and everyone knows that this is where rock 'n' roll *really* began.

Well, everybody should, but most people don't. Driving past dilapidated juke joints and roadhouses, I'm reminded of the Rolling Stones concert in New Jersey where I almost came to blows with the yuppie scum in the seat behind mine. It was the last night of the *Steel Wheels* tour, and there had been rumors that Eric Clapton might join them onstage. Except for the fact that he was a Yardbird, that didn't really do much for me, but I was at a Stones show so I wasn't going to complain about anything. Not so the two khaki-wearers in row F.

"All right, New Jersey! We've got another special guest for you," Jagger announced from the stage, and the khakis high-fived each other.

"It's Clapton," they yelled jubilantly, cheering and whistling until the guest appeared and was decidedly not Eric Clapton.

"Who the fuck is that?" One of them spat as an elderly, stooped black man in an orange suit and hat was led to a stool in the center of the stage. "What the hell?"

"Ladies and gentleman, John Lee Hooker!"

"Who?" Before I even had time to be outraged, the other khaki followed up with this: "I know I didn't pay fifty dollars to see some rickety old nigger."

I wanted to say something. I wanted to say *"there wouldn't be a Rolling Stones or an Eric Clapton without John Lee Hooker."* I wanted to say *"neither one of you guys is fit to lick John Lee Hooker's boots!"* But I didn't say anything. I watched John Lee Hooker sing "Boogie Chillun" and I felt like crying, I was so pissed off. Fuckers. They didn't deserve to be in the same room with John Lee Hooker *or* the Rolling Stones. As usual, the men don't know, but the little girls understand.

And the Doors didn't write that, by the way. Willie Dixon did.

✝

I pull into Oxford, Mississippi, just before bedtime and
take a room in the Old Miss Motel. I pick up a copy of *USA
Today*, a box of Fig Newtons, and a Coke at the market
down the street and hole up for the night, watching prime
time and eating cookies. As I'm flipping through the paper
looking for a crossword, a cheesy graph catches my eye. It's
ranking the cost of a cheeseburger, fries, and a drink in different cities around the country. I look for Athens, but of
course it's not there, an also-ran in world economics. Los
Angeles, of course, is leading the pack with a total of
$12.63. Twelve dollars for a cheeseburger! One thing I had
made sure not to tell my parents before I left was that my
high school journalism teacher told us the average income
for freelance writers was $5,000 a year. I scribble the math
in the newspaper margin. Well, heck. I could get four hundred cheeseburgers for that. Until I remember things like
rent and clothes, I am heartened. I roll up the sleeve on the
rest of my Fig Newtons and stick them in my backpack.
I'm probably going to need to save them for Los Angeles.

The next morning, I walk over to the university library
where the blues archive is housed. I figure the presence of
actual artifacts from Howlin' Wolf, Muddy Waters, and
maybe even Robert Johnson will cleanse any remaining
paisley stains from my soul. Will they have instruments?
Will I be able to actually listen to any recordings? My own
blues collection consists of a stack of Sonny Boy Williamson reissues and a Robert Johnson box set, but I am

nothing if not eager to learn. I plan to spend the whole day at the archive. Or planned to, until Evil Blues Librarian gives me the blues good and proper by refusing to even let me in.

"You need to have a specific research purpose in order to access the archive," she sniffs prissily, peering at me from behind smudgy lenses. Her mouseburger gray-brown hair is cut in that triangular chin-length pageboy that looks so at home among ivory towers and special collections, and, just in case you didn't know she was true academe, around her neck hangs the hallmark of the female scholar—the art necklace. A thickly corded, chest-length mishmash of oddly shaped glass beads, fetishes, and metal bits, it fairly cries "Don't fuck with me, missy, I've got *tenure*."

"A purpose other than wanting to learn about the history of the blues?" What more noble purpose could there be, I wonder, than love of the music and a desire to be closer to its source?

"A *specific research* purpose," she reiterates. If I'd had any poison on me, I would have Robert Johnsoned her coffee right there.

"Look," I say, hoping to appeal to the nerd in her, which has gotta be awfully big since she is, after all, a research librarian at a university, and don't forget that necklace, "I drove down here from Richmond, Virginia, to see the blues archive." I conveniently leave out the part about Los Angeles and hair metal and Elvis. Like they teach you in writing class, you don't want to muck up the plot with too many details. "I drove through five states to see this stuff, and you're telling me I can't see it because I don't have a good enough reason?"

"You don't have *any* reason," she corrects me and closes the logbook.

"And you don't have *any* soul," I spit back. I leave, dejected, but not before stopping mid-slink to take a picture of Sonny Boy Williamson's actual harmonica, housed in a glass case at the library door. *Fuckin' Sonny Boy, man, I came to see you*, I think, gazing wistfully through the glass. I wonder what Sonny Boy and Howlin' Wolf would think if they could see us now, anyway—a couple of nerdy white chicks fighting over them. The blues probably never thought it would end up locked in a library, accessible only to elite scholars. *Fuck a library,* I think. What do they know from rock 'n' roll?

The nasty run-in with the blues librarian almost makes me want to blow off my one academic side trip, but after stewing over it on the walk to the car I realize that William Faulkner would have thought she was a raging bitch, too. I decide to go visit him in spite of my burgeoning resentment against Ole Miss. Besides, Faulkner wasn't an academic, he was a *badass.* I follow my map to the cemetery on the north side of town, and, after scouting around the grounds for a good bit, find the final resting place of Count No Count himself. I bring no pageantry, no flowery speeches, and no pretentious bottles of wine with me on my visit; I'm just paying a southern social call to say, "Hey, man, you were pretty damn good." I grab a couple of photos and dust the Mississippi mud off his marker as best I can, wondering what kind of advice ol' Bill would have for me if he were here. Probably something gruff and hard-bitten, like don't suffer fools or keep your cards covered. I hope that I am

hard-bitten enough to make it in the big city, as it were, and
as I sit with my back against William Faulker's headstone,
I resolve to keep my cards covered and suffer no fools from
here on out. After a languid hour of reflection and meditation, hoping to absorb some of Faulkner's writing talent
and fame by osmosis, but hopefully not the accompanying
alcoholism and bouts with electroshock, it's off to Memphis
where the King awaits.

✝

In Memphis, I figure I can go for the proverbial two birds
and eat lunch at Sun Studio, because they have a restaurant
there—or rather, they *are* a restaurant there, right where
Elvis used to record. I could spend a long time lamenting
the state of a world where the birthplace of some of the
most important music of our generation is whored out as a
kitschy rockola-style tourist trap, but I am just happy to be
here, and besides, I'm hungry. Man does not live on rocka-
billy alone; man needs meatloaf, and iced tea, and peanut-
butter-and-banana sandwiches. You know Elvis would have
agreed. After gratefully checking out of my hellhole of a
motel—and pausing to take a few pictures of it from the
safety of my car—I drive down to Sun, where I order
myself up a nanner sammich and a tall glass of milk.

I can feel the sandwich making me more rock 'n' roll
with every bite. I try and concentrate on the experience so
I'll always remember it. *I'm eating Elvis's favorite sandwich in
Elvis's recording studio.* I wonder if he ever ate a nanner sammich here? Probably not, but I'll bet he wanted to. If there

was one here, well, he definitely would have. That works for me. I finish my lunch and take a walk around the studio, peering into the one preserved studio and trying to feel the presence of the greats move through me. In truth, though, I feel more at one with the spirit when I see the Sun Records T-shirt on the wall over the cash register.

Q: *What's the big deal? It's just a T-shirt, isn't it?*

A: *For the uninitiated, the Sun Records T-shirt is the official uniform of the truly cool. Like the CBGB T-shirt, the Sun Records T-shirt is always black—only black—and is usually seen with Levi's, boots, and either a denim jacket or a leather jacket. Wearing one is like knowing a secret handshake or having an Ovaltine decoder ring—it's a message to other hipsters that you are a hipster, too. You can buy Sun Records shirts online, and you can buy CBGB shirts at Hot Topic now, but it's my personal belief that you shouldn't be allowed to wear either shirt unless you—or someone you actually know—purchased it in person at Sun Records or CBGB. You can't buy cool online, and you sure as hell can't buy it at Hot Topic. On this same subject, when I see teenagers at the mall wearing Sid Vicious T-shirts, I think that it would be entirely fair for me to demand that they sing me the first verse of "Anarchy in the UK." If they can't do that, I should be allowed to kick them in the shins.*

Needless to say, I have to buy a Sun Records T-shirt. After all, what else will I wear when I am photographed hobnobbing backstage with Guns N' Roses after I become the most in-demand freelancer on the Sunset Strip? I imagine

myself in my Sun Records shirt and Levi's, looking effort-
lessly cool and somehow very tall and skinny (hey, it's my
fantasy). I'm chuckling wryly and sharing a witty story
with Axl and Slash, who hang on my every word. Yes, I
have to have that T-shirt.

Except I've left my credit card in the car. I have a ten
in my pocket, but that's not enough for the lunch and the
shirt, so I need to make a quick trip outside. After the
laconic gray-haired cashier gets my shirt out of the cabinet
for me, I hand him the ten and ask him to hold it while I go
to the car.

"Now, why would I want to do sum'n lahk that?" he
drawls from beneath his brushy mustache, waving the
money away as if he were swatting at a lazy fly.

"Well, because I already ate lunch and I haven't paid
for it. You know, so you can make sure I don't skip out on
the tab."

His eyes crinkle with amusement, and he shrugs.
"You're the one's got to live with yourself if you do."

I take back the ten, chastened, and walk out to my car
wondering how I'm going to manage when I leave the
south. Then I come back, because I have to live with
myself, and if I don't have a Sun Records T-shirt to wear in
Los Angeles, I will surely die.

Shirt in hand and sandwich in belly, I arrive at Graceland serene and full of the spirit, or at least of peanut but-
ter and bananas. I buy my ticket and attach myself to a
group of European tourists about to head inside. Camera at
the ready, I prepare to document my experience room by
room. A perky brunette tour guide who looks for all the

world like Shelley Fabares in *Girl Happy* herds us into the
living room, and for a moment I think it's all been a dream,
because this can't be Elvis's living room. It looks just like
my Aunt Ida's living room, down to the last framed family
portraits on the glass end table! Well, except for the over-
whelmingly garish stained-glass peacocks flanking the door,
that is. But honestly, the thing that is the most striking
about Elvis's living room is how incredibly rock 'n' roll it is
not. Really, it looks like an old lady living room—which,
once I think about it, makes sense, because if there is anything Elvis wanted to do his whole life it was please his
mama. This living room is Gladys all the way. I snap pictures furiously, making sure to capture details like the
miniature Greek goddess ensconced in a hurricane lamp.
That about says it all when it comes to Elvis's decor.

The dining room is more Gladys—candelabras, china
whatnots, cranberry glass jars, and a huge chandelier drip-
ping with crystal overwhelming the small room. *Click.
Clickclickclick.* We move into the hallway and I stop to stare
at a toddler photo of Lisa Marie, hanging in the mirrored
stairwell (yes, mirrored stairwell). *Click.* But we don't get
to go upstairs, because Elvis's Aunt Delta still lives at
Graceland and we've got to respect her privacy. Elvis's
Aunt Delta! No way! Can we meet her? No, of course not,
don't be silly, move along, please. We head down to the
basement to check out Elvis's TV room.

In the basement, I say a silent prayer of thanks that I
did not die in the seventies and have everything I wore and
every room I decorated in 1977-era style preserved as a
standing monument to my life. If that had been the case,

people would be touring my green shag-carpeted room, their eyes tormented by my lavender bunk beds and matching beanbag chairs, all set off perfectly by the floral vinyl wallpaper in Easter egg hues. Let me be even clearer: Elvis was a styling motherfucker. Fifties Elvis in jeans and work-shirts, sixties Elvis in black leather and sideburns—it's all good. But seventies Elvis? White jumpsuits and scarves, butterfly collars and rhinestones . . . and this room. This godawful nightmare of a room. Elvis's TV room looks like a rejected set from the *Electric Company*—black, yellow, and white with a huge cloud and lightning bolt painted on the wall. What was it with lightning bolts in the seventies? Did the whole world lapse into an unexplained period of Zeus worship for a decade? The room is horrific. I'm thrilled when we're escorted out of the basement.

We're not allowed to go into the kitchen, because that's part of Aunt Delta's lair, and that truly disappoints me because to me Elvis and kitchens go hand in hand. I want to see the room where the nanner sammiches were made, the pork chops were cooked, and the ice cream sundaes were concocted on a whim for breakfast. I want to see the source of his corpulence and stand in the same room where I know Elvis stood in the middle of the night on a search for tasty treats. I try to peek in as they lead us past on our way to the jungle room, and I'm admonished by Shelley Fabares to "*please* stay with the group" for the third time on the tour. Can I help it if I need longer to soak up the holiness? Besides, it's the details I'm checking out, the whatnots and ashtrays, what pictures are on the end tables and what books are on the shelves. I don't care about the gold records on the wall; I want to see what Elvis was doing when he was home alone and bored on a rainy Tuesday morning.

I forge ahead and catch up to the tour, though, because it's time to see the jungle room, which is what everyone talks about when they talk about touring Graceland. *Oh, the jungle room, it's so amazing, completely over the top, you just won't believe it,* they say, shaking their heads in awe, wonder, and something that almost looks like superiority. Yes, superiority, and this is the King of Rock 'n' Roll they're talking about. Well, to this I say *clambake* now that I personally have seen the jungle room up close and in person. Fake stone walls, tiki lamps, and fur-upholstered chairs, not to mention the exact same green shag rug that my bedroom sported in 1977. I'm disappointed and find myself getting just a little pissed on Elvis's behalf. The jungle room is the ultimate 1970s rumpus room, complete with wet bar, and yes, styles have changed, so maybe it looks garish by our pedestrian standards, but Elvis didn't ask anybody to freeze it in time and lead tours through on the hour, now, did he? How *dare* a bunch of smart-ass rock-critic types use the tackiness of the jungle room to belittle the King? For all they know, if he'd lived, he'd be wearing paisley now and decorating in rocking Danish modern. Well, probably not, but he'd be cooler than them no matter what his sofa looked like. It's not his fucking fault he died in 1977.

My righteousness on behalf of my new best friend El is cut short by the beeping of a smoke alarm. A *smoke alarm*, so pedestrian and homey, here at Graceland. For a minute I don't even recognize what the beeps mean.

Shelley apologizes—"there are men working in the trophy room and they keep setting it off"—but fire codes being what they are, we have to evacuate. No problem for me, because in my ire over America's collective sneer at the decor of the jungle room, I started to feel a little ghoulish myself. Does Elvis want us walking around his house, staring at his things? Would he want me taking pictures of his whatnots? I hope in my heart that he realizes my motives are pure and that I'm not here to laugh and sneer at his tiki lamps. I just want to feel a little closer to him is all.

Bringing up the rear, as always, I stop on my way through the dining room to steal one last peek at the china cabinet when I notice motion back in the kitchen. Getting as close to the door as I dare (because really, what can they do now, throw me off the tour? It's over), I am rewarded with a quick glimpse of Elvis's Aunt Delta in all her house-coated glory, scurrying off, no doubt, to some secret fire exit or maybe just to grab a quick biscuit while we're all out on the front lawn. I feel as though I've had a vision, or that I've been given a sign, an omen blessing my rock 'n' roll future in Los Angeles. I have gazed on Aunt Delta with my own two eyes. I have been in the presence of a Presley. Hallelujah and thank'ya verrahmuch. I feel that now the trip has already been worthwhile, no matter what happens from here on out.

The rest of the day is inconsequential—after all, I have had a sighting of Presley kin. I take my pictures in the meditation garden where Elvis, Gladys, Vernon, and Grandma Minnie Mae are buried, and I add my name to the wall out front with the thousands of others in languages from around the globe, but it can't hold up to seeing Aunt Delta in living color.

I visit some souvenir stores on Elvis Presley Boulevard, picking up some T-shirts, coffee mugs, and a fringed velvet pillowcase for my best friend Melissa, whose Boston wedding I am missing even as we speak—linens are always an appropriate wedding gift, even for rocker chicks getting married in thrift-store dresses that show off their tattoos. Then I set out for my next scheduled destination: Tucson, Arizona, 1,400 miles away.

2

Confessions of a Reluctant Danzig Bimbo
"Sorry, Kid, We Don't Speak Irony"

he long, lonely stretch of highway between Memphis and Tucson gives me plenty of time to think about the inevitable fiasco that awaits me in L.A. No job, no apartment, not even a friend to show me around—what was I thinking? Well, I was thinking I was going to be the next Lester Bangs, but that's beside the point. The point is that I am almost there and now, suddenly, it all seems way too real. I distract myself with Suzi Quatro tapes and a one-pound bag of Twizzlers propped open on the passenger seat. With red licorice as my copilot, I shall overcome. Hauling ass across the southern states in my now very well-traveled Hyundai, I power open the sunroof, hoping to maybe add some highlights to my ready-for-L.A. body-waved hair. I was hoping for something along the lines of Tawny Kitaen but I ended up closer to Chaka Khan. Big hair is big hair, though, and mine is the biggest it's ever been. Tearing through the desert with Suzi blaring, I feel like I am finally living my rock 'n' roll dream, and it squashes my self-doubt into an almost imperceptible little nugget deep down in my subconscious.

At least I have a friendly face waiting for me in Tucson. Well, I hope so, anyway. I haven't seen Rachel since just after high school graduation, when she grew out her mohawk, went all macrobiotic on us, and took off to follow the Grateful Dead. Midway through the tour she fell in love with Avram Shulman, a rabbinical student and psychedelic rocker. They settled in Tucson, where Rachel inched toward a bachelor's degree and Avram balanced his fuzzbox dreams and Talmud studies with a day job embossing personalized pencil sets.

Rachel and I have kept up a steady correspondence over the years, based mostly on mutual complaining about the scenes at our conservative colleges and trading fliers for punk rock shows in Richmond and Tucson. Now, by happy coincidence, I'll actually be able to tour some of the clubs I've come to know through four years of long-distance fliers.

Rachel meets me at her front door in tie-dye and combat boots, both of the Rachels I remember crammed into one tiny four-foot-eleven package. It's just like old times immediately, and minutes after my arrival we are happily sipping jasmine tea in her tiny, cluttered kitchen, the have-you-heard-about-so-and-so patter occasionally interrupted by furtive taps at the back door. Each time the taps occur, Rachel pauses the conversation long enough to reach in the refrigerator for a wax-paper-wrapped burrito or peanut-butter sandwich from the bottom shelf, which she hands out the back door with a quick *"de nada."*

"Illegals," she explains without really explaining. I would expect nothing less. I regale Rachel with tales of my trip so far, and of my plans for taking L.A. by storm with my nouveau Lester Bangsian greatness. Even though she's hardly a metalhead, Rachel is the most supportive of my plans of anyone so far. It's the whole hippie follow-your-bliss thing, seasoned with a sprinkle of good old punk rock "fuck 'em if they don't like it." We talk well into the night, until Avram comes home from a show he'd promoted for the Marshmallow Overcoat, a band I remember from Rachel's faithful flier collecting ("Try On the Marshmallow Overcoat!"). Rachel had already warned me about Avram's crippling shyness, so I do my best not to overwhelm him with greetings and glad-handing. Besides, by that time, I've been up for a good twenty hours, so I gratefully accept my pillow and linens and head for the couch for some shut-eye.

Aside from the requisite psychedelic club-hopping, my weeklong stay in Tucson is decidedly laid back. Rachel and I spend our days prowling thrift shops and eating at taquerias, and our off-nights drinking beer in a series of seedy dives around her and Avram's equally seedy apartment. Sometimes Avram joins us, but usually he stays home with his sixties records and Hebrew texts. On one such night, we come home to find Avram uncharacteristically animated, waiting to fill us in on the fantastic score he'd made while we were down at the corner reminiscing over pitchers of draft beer. It seems that somewhere between *Shoftim* and *Yeshaya*, he had managed to be the seventh caller to KXCI and won himself two tickets to see Danzig tomorrow night at the El Casino Ballroom.

For the uninitiated, Danzig is just about *the* boo-spook-iest prepube metal band on the metal scene. Long shunned by MTV for such video antics as, say, ripping a chicken in half over the stomach of a scantily clad babe laid out on an altar under a crucified demon, Danzig is shopping-mall horror at its cheesiest. Lead singer Glenn Danzig is a five-foot-three bundle of deltoids, leather, and Lady Clairol Midnight Black, a role model for every pencil-necked middle school misfit who ever devoured *The Necronomicon* in study hall. Speaking of misfits, if Danzig looks familiar, it's because Glenn fronted the seminal punk band the Misfits in the late 1970s and early '80s. The Misfits' "Fiend Club" grinning skull logo is the Lacoste gator of the skateboards-and-mohawks set, tempting me occasionally to grab the odd fiend-sporting suburban teenage wannabe from his seat at the Chesterfield Mall food court and demand he hum a few bars of a Misfits song so I can slap him when he can't, just like the Hot Topic kids, and besides, where do you think he got that Misfits shirt? But I digress. The Misfits are no more. Danzig is the new Black Messiah. And now we are going to see him. Well, two of us are, anyway.

"You go with Avram," Rachel insists. "I have physics homework."

"But he's your boyfriend; he'll want you to go."

"I don't want to see Danzig," Rachel says, pulling a leftover tofu pup out of the fridge and dabbing it with hot sauce. She has a point.

"But we won't have fun without you," I plead, not adding that I find shy Avram hopelessly difficult to talk to, a problem compounded by a situation that very morning in which I, thinking both of my hosts had already left the house, wandered naked and glassesless out of the shower and ran smack into a traumatized Avram in the hallway.

"Well, I'm between a hard rock and a stone." Rachel is

not an English major. "I'd really rather not. You and Avram will have fun. He never goes to these things; it will be a learning experience for him. Do it as a favor. You guys can dress up and try to blend in."

After sleeping on Rachel's suggestion, I reluctantly agree to go with Avram. The concept of turning it into an exercise in irony does actually take a little bit of the pressure off me, plus it appeals to my pretentious smartass side, which I need to be cultivating anyway if the rock critics I grew up reading are any kind of example.

That night, in preparation for the show, I tease and spray my Chaka Khan hair until it resembles the tumbleweeds I passed on Interstate 40 on the way into town and don my black leather skirt and matching push-up bra. With fishnet stockings and stiletto spikes, it is truly an outfit with which to be reckoned. I have only worn it on two other occasions because it always seems to attract the wrong element. Slut fashion notwithstanding, we still need to keep out the riffraff.

Presently Avram arrives home from his job at the pencil factory. I wobble into the living room and do a runway twirl on my spikes. "Gee," he says, and goes into the kitchen. I get the distinct impression that Avram isn't used to concertwear that isn't drapey and caftanish. Rachel looks hard at me. She rips a corner off her physics homework and scribbles her phone number on it.

"This is in case anything *happens,*" she says ominously. "Call me if there's *an emergency.*"

"Oh, come on," I groan, poking my hair up another three inches. "What's gonna happen?"

Rachel reaches over and adjusts the straps on my bra. "I don't know," she says, shaking her head.

Avram disappears into the bedroom and eventually emerges wearing a purple paisley shirt and bellbottom jeans. Peering down at our lemony faces, he submits to our fashion dominance and in short order is decked out in leather pants (mine), a Cramps T-shirt (Rachel's), and a top hat. The lid is his own, surprisingly; if psychedelia and heavy metal were graphed on a Venn diagram, the overlap would be fairly substantial—at least from the neck up. With his jewfro brushed out and the hat pushed down, he actually looks kinda like Slash. Slash with Coke-bottle glasses and a honkin' big nose, but kinda like Slash all the same.

With emergency instructions in hand, Avram and I proceed to the El Casino Ballroom. Danzig is just starting their set when we arrive. Glenn Danzig seems about to collapse under the weight of his own musculature. The man's shoulders start round about the tops of his ears. He closely resembles a pit bull—a damn fine-looking pit bull. I may have my tongue firmly in cheek with the outfit, and I may snicker at the giant demon head hanging above the stage, but make no mistake, I love me some Glenn Danzig biceps. I lead Avram to the edge of the mosh pit, a teeming mass of sweaty bodies and overactive hormones. Dozens of urgent-looking teenaged boys are hurling themselves against one another with amazing force, like crazed, testosterone-driven atoms with bad skin.

"Exhibit A—the mosh pit," I shout above the din. Avram peers at the flailing bodies from behind his wire-rimmed glasses and backs up a step. I lead him around the edge of the mosh pit to the front row. A pocket of fabulous babes are clustered at stage right, making doe eyes at Glenn Danzig as he declares that he is the Killer Wolf and he is gonna pound them home. Several apes from the road crew ogle the babes from behind the Marshall stacks, elbowing one another and licking their chops.

"Exhibit B—sluts," I say, meaning it of course in a wholesome family way and intending no slight against the character of aforementioned sluts. Avram looks at a red-bra-clad blonde with two nose rings and backs up two steps.

Just then a violent mosh sends us lurching sideways. I grab the edge of the stage and hang on, riding the wave for all I'm worth. One of the roadies reaches over, I assume to pry my grubby paws off his precious stage. I raise my hands in a sign-language apology—*sorry there, Bucky, didn't mean to touch your stage*—and discover that I am now holding a red satin sticker that reads "LONG WAY BACK FROM HELL—LUCIFUGE WORLD TOUR: GUEST." Yes, I am now in proud possession of my very own Slut Pass. I'd be lying if I said I wasn't a little bit impressed with myself, irony notwithstanding. I may be joking around about this outfit, but the fact that someone's actually buying it is flattering, in a nonironic, ego-boosting kinda way.

I turn around and show Avram the Slut Pass. He checks out the spooky font, the shiny satin, the silkscreen of an upside-down cross dangling on Glenn Danzig's bare chest.

"Gee," he says.

We scrutinize the pass together, wondering how I,

rather than an actual slut, came to receive it. Avram squints myopically at the crowd, the roadies, the band.

"They must have picked you out for Dan. I think you guys are the same height."

"Dan?"

"Didn't you say he was the singer? Dan Zig?" Sometimes I can't tell whether Avram is really kidding.

Q: *So is this your first-ever Slut Pass?*

A: *At the risk of impugning my own character, which heretofore I am sure you all considered sterling, no, it is not. My first Slut Pass was bequeathed to me and my partner in crime Claudia Arnold by a roadie for none other than the Clash, in 1983, when I was fifteen years old, sporting a fresh peroxide job, tight army pants, and a red bandanna tied around my left combat boot. For one shining night, I was practically Lester Bangs, or at least Sable Starr. I got groped by a photographer, screeched at jealously by Ellen Foley (who was dating Mick Jones at the time but who the more mainstream among you may remember as the female voice in Meatloaf's "Paradise by the Dashboard Light"), and grounded for pretty much the rest of the school year for cutting class, taking a Greyhound bus to Williamsburg, and then having the nerve to call Claudia's father at two A.M. to pick us up. On a school night. And the Clash? Perfect gentlemen.*

Now that we've seen the view from the front, and now that I've got the Slut Pass (Exhibit C), I guide Avram around the ballroom, pointing out some of the more important elements of a good heavy metal show—tattoos, nipple rings, underage kids getting loaded. Without discussing it, we are both content not to try and fight our way back up front. I figure there's no point risking injury to get up close and personal if I'm going to be meeting the band anyway, and Avram, well, I think Avram is scared. Maybe of the mosh pit, or maybe of Dan Zig and his pointed nails and massive biceps. Whatever the cause, he looks like he is more than content to hang out at the back of the ballroom for as long as I will let him.

When the band finishes their standard set, and before the crowd brings them out for the obligatory (and thereby utterly meaningless, in my opinion) encore, I head for the ladies' room to make sure I look trampy enough to take the heat in the metal-slut kitchen. Before I go, we discuss the possibility of trying to slide Avram under the umbrella of the pass with me, an offer that Avram declines so heartily that his top hat flies off. Instead, Avram agrees to wait for me in the parking lot after the show until the backstage festivities are over. That's what I like about Avram. He's an agreeable kind of guy.

A quick look around the bathroom is all it takes to indoctrinate me into the workings of the concert slut caste system. Studiously avoiding the restrooms at concerts is my norm, so this is a new and wondrous world to me, and suddenly I am a part of it. I can't believe my good fortune—at least I think it's good fortune. There is definitely a pyramid here, and I am pleased to see that, for one of the few times in my life, I am not at the bottom of it. That is where one finds the *Chicks*. Chicks are the T-shirt-wearing, ticket-buying, lighter-waving party girls. Some are cute, some are not—it doesn't really matter. They didn't come to the concert to impress anybody; they came to have a good time. And they didn't come into the bathroom to primp; they came in to pee. Once that's done, they leave. Nothing wrong with being a Chick. In fact, if Joan Jett, Suzi Quatro, and Runaways-era Lita Ford were here, they would all fall firmly into the Chick category.

Just above Chicks in the hierarchy are the Passless Sluts. The middle class of metal sluttery, perhaps they didn't quite rate, or maybe they just weren't spotted by the right roadie. They've got the clothes, the hair, and the makeup, but they lack the all-important satin square. They stand at the mirrors above the sinks and primp, all the while glaring at the Backstage Betties.

That would be my group, the Betties. The girls with the passes hog the full-length mirror and bogart the makeup table, and *nobody* tells us to hurry up at the sink. The Betties speak only to one another, occasionally casting scornful glances at the no-passers. They lend each other lip pencils and help out with those tough back zippers, showing a sisterly camaraderie that will no doubt fall by the wayside once backstage. At least, I assume it will. One would think that it has to. In any case, I can't wait to find out.

I take advantage of my newfound power and spread out my Slut ammo on the makeup table. A little more mascara, a little more contour powder, and a lot more cleavage—I may be a slut, but I'm not a *dumb* slut. I know how I rated this pass. Several of the other Betties are in various stages of undress in the drafty restroom, and the scene takes on a conspiratorial air.

"My mother would *shit,*" exclaims a small blonde girl to no one in particular as she wriggles her bare butt into a crimson leather dress. "I mean, she'd *die*. I had to smuggle this out in my *boot*." She rolls up her jeans and T-shirt and stuffs them behind the trash can. I notice that her pass is different from the rest of ours—it's *laminated*, meaning she's a notch above us, even. I can't imagine how *that* merit badge is earned. You'd have to sell a hell of a lot of cookies, that's for sure.

Another girl is grunting and groaning as she tries to refasten the back hooks on her studded bra after a major boob adjustment. "Hey, help me with this, will ya?" she pleads. I dutifully do her up, and she turns around. She looks about twelve. She adjusts her nonexistent cleavage with both hands and nods in my direction. "Thanks a lot. That bottom hook is a motherfucker, ain't it?"

Sisterhood aside, the bathroom experience is making me feel fat, and plain, and suddenly very *old*. At twenty-three, I'm one of the senior Betties present, and a lot of these chicks are acting like this is just another night, one more rock star, one more dressing room, one more day in a life that plays out like one long Warrant video. I hate my life! I hate my chubby thighs and Snoopy nose and four years wasted in college when I should have been prowling for rock stars! Damn these girls! Where are their parents, and why aren't they keeping a better eye on them? I don't need the competition! I can see the ending now, with me muttering like the villain in a Scooby Doo cartoon— "Glenn Danzig? Yeah! I could've had him, too, if it hadn't been for those meddling kids!" I continue dutifully helping with zippers and sharing mascara, barely containing my burgeoning resentment against my new best friends.

Self-pitying interlude completed, I pack up my tools and charge out of the restroom loaded for bear. In the Ballroom, my self-esteem is resuscitated by the number of envious glances I notice aimed at my satin square. Back straight, I nudge the passless peons out of the way and strut over to a roadie.

"Excuse me," I say, tapping him on the shoulder. He turns around and stares straight down between my breasts for a full ten seconds. Impatiently, I duck down so that I am staring him in the eye and wave my backstage pass at him.

"Could you please tell me where the sluts are supposed to go?"

He looks at me a little funny but points me in the direction of the backstage door. Several of the other sluts are already there, along with a few guys who look to be record store cashiers or college DJs—you know the look: "I make minimum wage, collect action figures, and live in my mother's basement, but man, am I *cool*."

I take my place in the growing queue of sycophantic hopefuls. There we stand, waiting for our audience with the Satanic Studmuffin and the lesser of the evils, Eerie, John, and Chuck. Eyeing one of the record store clerks, I am reminded of a visit to Harmony Hut the summer before I started high school. Delighted to find a copy of Johnny Thunders's *So Alone*, I handed over eight dollars of my hard-earned babysitting money to a Ric Ocasek look-alike who sneered, "I thought little girls your age were supposed to listen to Rick Springfield." (I didn't think of the perfect comeback until I was halfway through the mall: "I thought old men your age were supposed to make more than four dollars an hour.") After a while, a manager type sticks his head out of the dressing room and looks around. A few of the College DJs make a break for the door, but the guy waves them off.

"Just the ladies for now, please! Only the girls!"

In we herd, wagging our tails behind us. I had been hoping to stand back and observe the bacchanal sociologically, from a distance, but in the tiny dressing room, there are no neutral corners. The other Betties are mobbing Glenn Danzig over by the buffet table, so I sneak past and position myself atop the wardrobe chest, behind a rack of shiny black clothes. Looking down, I see that I am not alone. Bassist Eerie Von is sitting in the corner, putting on his boots.

"Hi," I say, for lack of anything more original.

"Hello." Eerie does not look up. He seems intent on avoiding the entire fleshfest. Thus snubbed, I return to my observations.

Guitarist John Christ and drummer Chuck Biscuits are sitting on folding metal chairs against a far wall, talking to a roadie about the inferior sound system at the Ballroom. They don't seem too offended at being ignored by the swarming sluts. Peering around the comely mob, I see that Glenn looks none too upset about the situation himself. He's signing body parts and posing for Polaroids with his arm around each girl. He looks less like the Antichrist than a somewhat sweaty, tattooed, leather-clad Care Bear—Beelze-Bear. I'm disappointed but at the same time relieved to see that there is a very regimented feel to the

Betty-greeting process here. Where the Clash's dressing room was more like a free-for-all party, this seems more like a receiving line at a wedding reception. My fears of being tossed aside as a pretender and an inferior specimen wane with the realization that, for Danzig, this is all business. With that realization in mind, I get the brilliant idea that instead of flirting, I could *schmooze!* The first schmooze of the trip! I take a deep breath and try and switch over from Bettie mode to schmooze mode.

As I prepare myself for the schmooze and the girls depart one by one with their snapshots, I am able to get a clearer view of the buffet table. Well, at least this should be good, I think. Surely Mister Lucifuge will have something sinister on his rider, something gory and shriek-worthy. Something to write home about. Raw meat? Lamb's hearts? Sour mash drunk from a virgin's skull? I scan the length of the table hopefully. At one end there are dozens of bottles of Snapple, all flavors, iced down in a large tub. Lining the rest of the length of the table are several silver, cauldron-sized bowls. The first contains pretzels. The second, M&Ms. The third is full of Reese's Cups, and the final bowl is brimming with . . . Gummi Bears.

I slide down from the wardrobe chest and move closer, to be sure. Yes. Gummi Bears. Hardly the type of fare one would expect from the man who wrote "Brains at every single meal / Can't we please have some guts." I keep an eye on the bowl, hoping that Glenn will at least spear some of the little bears with his pointy fingernails and chomp 'em down, but no such luck. In fact, none of the band touches any of the food.

I glance back toward the corner and see that Eerie's been discovered. The red-bra-and-nose-rings slut from the front row has him cornered against the wardrobe chest. She's talking a mile a minute about a green velvet dress that cost her seventy dollars in Phoenix. Eerie seems very interested in the hinge on his folding chair.

"Really . . . seventy dollars," he is saying as he examines the hinge.

I watch Eerie try to blow the girl off for an agonizing five minutes before I notice that Glenn Danzig is making his way around the room and he's headed my way. Ever the gentleman, he's introducing himself to all of the assembled beauties, shaking hands, and generally giving good schmooze. I estimate that I have another three minutes to decide how I want to play my big chance. Realistic about my Betty ranking—I'm definitely looking at "Miss Congeniality" at best, given the competition. What I really hope to do is schmooze like hell, make an impression, and maybe come out of this with one juicy contact, one name, one number, one industry guy, magazine editor, or *somebody* I can call when I get to L.A. and say, just casually, "by the way, I was in Danzig's dressing room a couple of weeks ago and Glenn says hey." I watch him moving down the line, kissing Betties, shaking hands, smiling and nodding as he pretends to enjoy himself. I try and think of a snappy opening comment but it's no use; I think the leather bra is cutting off the oxygen supply to my brain. Sidetracked, it occurs to me that maybe that's the problem with all Betties . . . maybe they are all rocket scientists when dressed in less constrictive clothing. God knows I can barely put sentences together with my boobs cinched up this tight.

And then it happens. Suddenly I'm shaking hands with the Prince of Darkness himself. Avram was right; he's about my height, and less scary up close. He's handsome, in that lantern-jawed super-villain way, but almost shy, lowering his head and looking up as he greets me in a hoarse Jersey voice.

"Hey, how ya doin'?"

"Great, thanks. Hey, I *loved* the Misfits." Stupid, stupid, *stupid!* I might as well have said "What was *that* crap?"

Glenn is gracious, but does let a slight eye roll slide past. It's not until later that I find out he's not speaking to Jerry and Doyle any more.

"Yeah, thanks." He looks fidgety, like he's waiting for me to do something, say something, produce something for him to sign. I need to move fast. I lean in and start blathering.

"Hey, uh, actually, I don't really *live* here, I'm just visiting, and, well, I'm really on my way to Los Angeles because Steve Peters from *Metal* magazine . . ." Glenn tilts his head, looks puzzled. Shit! I'm losing him! I cut to the chase. "Well, anyway, I'm trying to write for some magazines and I was just kinda wondering, and, like, maybe you know, uh, who is a good person to talk to?"

Glenn looks thoughtful, crinkles up his face like he's thinking, and then shrugs his massive shoulders at me.

"I don't know, who?"

Huh? Did he think I had asked him a riddle? I tactfully rephrase the question.

"No, I'm just asking *you* . . . you know, in case you know . . . like a magazine, an editor . . . who's good?"

"Oh, man, I don't know." He shrugs again. "There's lots of 'em out there, though. Good luck!" And that's the end of my audience. It's over, and I scored not so much as a Scooby Snack. Dummy, dummy, *dummy!* I am mentally kicking myself with stiletto spikes, which hurts even though they are figurative. Why didn't I make myself more understandable? Why didn't I ask him something really scintillating that would have made him stop greeting other Betties and stay and talk? Then I could have pumped him for contacts, asked for an internship, something. Instead I just *confused* him. And I blew it. Big time. I feel my nerd level rising in spite of my video bimbo attire.

As I am berating myself, the crowd in the dressing room is thinning out. It looks like the satanic orgy I had been hoping to witness is not going to happen. I wonder how Avram is doing in the parking lot. I help myself to a few Gummi Bears and slip outside. Avram is exactly where he said he would be, the prince.

Half an hour after the show has ended, there are still several dozen diehards hanging around by the band's tour bus. Avram and I decide to wait and see what happens when the band comes out. We are interested to see which of the Betties the band will pick to take on the bus. I'm wondering if Red Bra is going to pass; I'm betting at the very least that she's not going with Eerie.

After another fifteen minutes or so, the backstage door opens, and the band, Betties, and roadies pour into the parking lot. To my intense confusion, the roadies and Betties scatter, and the band hurls itself directly into the crush of teenaged fans surrounding the bus.

I think at first they are just trying to shove their way through and get the hell on the bus, but that is not the case. Once at the center of the crowd, they whip out their Sharpies and it's autograph time all over again. They don't quit until every kid in the crowd has four signatures and a photo if he wants one. For the kids, who have been waiting patiently since the show ended, this is obviously the best moment of all of their lives. I've never seen such awestruck faces on a bunch of baby-faced little satanists, and the band takes the time to meet and greet each and every dark little one of them. Such nice boys. Having thus satisfied all pressing social obligations, Danzig boards their bus—alone—and takes off for Irvine.

As we are leaving, curiosity gets the better of me. I capture a roadie who looks about fifteen and make up a lie.

"Hey, dude, have you seen my friend around? She's got on a red bra and two nose rings."

He nods. "She's on the crew bus."

"Are they taking her to California?"

He shakes his head and snorts. "Nahhhh . . . they'll be done with her any minute now."

I guess I might have figured, but I can't help but be a little taken aback. So this is what it's all for. We dress ourselves up in seventy-dollar velvet dresses and red bras and for what? So we can spend twenty minutes in the back of a bus with a tenth-grade dropout who can lift heavy things.

As I'm contemplating the sad reality of life's injustices, the bus door hisses open and Red Bra emerges. She's got her spike heels in her hand and a dazed look on her teenaged face. She looks around the parking lot as if she's never been there before. Catching sight of the satin square stuck to my leather skirt, she grins crookedly and gives me a conspiratorial wave. I wave back—we sluts stick together. She lets out a howl and waves her shoes in the air.

"Rock 'n' *rolllllllllllllll!"* she cries, and takes off running barefoot across the gravel parking lot.

3

Strippers, Clown Rooms, and Danzig Among the Mangoes
Day Jobs and Night Moves on Hollywood and Vine

he very first thing that jumps out at me about Los Angeles is not the highways, or the gang members, or the Hollywood sign looming down over the hills like a cheesy postcard. No, the first thing I notice is the embarrassment of would-be hair-metal gods looming large around every corner. If I were to say that you could not drive to the drugstore without shooing the hair-metal gods out of the way, you would probably think that I was merely being metaphorical. Try telling that to the hair-metal god who took his sweet time crossing against the light in front of my car, with turquoise necklaces draped across his bare romance-novel chest and leather pants glistening in the California sun, when all I wanted was for him to move his ass so I could get to the drugstore and get some Sine-Aid.

Hollywood is lousy with hair-metal gods because in every city, every small town, and every scene in America, there is that one band that is just a little too big for their small-town pond. Their singer is a little more flamboyant, their guitarist a little more well-muscled, and their chops a tiny bit more polished than the rest of the bands on their circuit. Sooner or later, this band, pumped full of the adulation that has been showered upon them in whatever corner of the country they call home, becomes convinced that

they are ready for the big time and decides to take Hollywood by storm. They have a big farewell concert, their
local paper runs a feature story with a big color photo, and
they load up the Econoline and head for the Sunset Strip—
where they are chagrined to find that they are now in
direct competition with every other "best band in town"
for the same few pay-for-play gigs. Any scholar of supply
and demand can tell you how this story ends. I can tell you
myself, because it is on my first day in Hollywood that I see
the final scene for myself. Strutting down Hollywood
Boulevard, in black stretch jeans and a zebra-striped shirt,
is a poodle-haired Poison look-alike . . . pushing a shopping
cart full of empty cans.

Lest I end up with my own can-filled cart, I figure I'd
better get to finding housing posthaste. Needless to say, my
parents shot down my original plan to get a room by the
week in the cheapest Hollywood motel I could find (think
Tom Waits), and instead made arrangements for me to stay
with friends from Saint Anthony's, which is, I guess, as
close to in loco parentis as they could get from three thousand miles away. As grateful as I am for their hospitality,
I am embarrassed to be imposing; here I am, a total
stranger showing up after more than a decade since they'd
left Richmond and St. Anthony's behind for the west coast,
demanding a place to stay. I'm equally ashamed of caving
into my parents' wishes even this far from home. I'll bet
Lester Bangs didn't have to stay with people from his parents' church when he moved to Detroit.

Q: *Are you sure? Maybe he did.*

A: *Actually, I am sure. Lester Bangs and the rest of the CREEM staff lived in a big commune-style farmhouse, which boggles the mind because how cool would it be to live with the whole entire staff of CREEM including Lester Bangs? That said, Lester Bangs's parents were Jehovah's Witnesses, so even if he had had to live with their friends, it might not have been as cool as a CREEM commune but it would have made a damn interesting reality show.*

My first order of business, though, before I even think about finding an apartment, is to let the good folks at *Metal* know that I'm ready for my close-up now. With invitation in hand and visions of Lester Bangs in my head, I pull up in front of their offices on Hollywood Boulevard in my road-weary Hyundai. As I jockey my car into the parking space and check my teeth for lipstick, you might think I would be worrying about my credentials, or my knowledge of the local metal scene, or the questions they might ask of a potential freelancer. Instead, I've spent the whole drive from Tucson agonizing about what to wear.

Q: *What to wear? Are you serious? Do you think Lester Bangs was worried about what to wear?*

A: *Well, that opens up a whole lovely kettle of worms about gender bias and beauty standards and the fact that Lester Bangs could still get laid even though he basically looked like a walrus, but let a woman put on ten pounds and she's a pariah. However, I'm going to save that for a more tedious book.*

My Sun Records T-shirt isn't broken in enough to be presentable yet, and most of my clothes fairly scream

Richmond, Virginia, and are therefore utterly unsuitable. You scoff, but large, unrecoverable chunks of my life have been spent planning Entrance Outfits. For every milestone, every once-in-a-lifetime chance to finally be cool and show them all, I have had in my head the Perfect Entrance Outfit. Granted, it never plays out in real life the way it does in my head, but I make the plans all the same. Case in point: my first day at Open High School. At fourteen, wide-eyed and metal-mouthed, I was never quite cool enough to fit in the way I dreamed I would for all those years leading up to my less than grand entrance in 1981. I had been planning my Entrance Outfit literally for years, changing the clothes, the hairstyle, and the soundtrack to keep up with the cutting edge. For the entire summer before ninth grade, I practiced painting on my Entrance Face with Wet N' Wild makeup to the backbeat of Blondie and the B-52s. I imagined strolling in on the first day of school in a pink-and-black-striped stretch top, unseasonably warm leather pants, and black ankle boots, none of which I actually owned. Oh, and I would have a Pat Benatar haircut. Her music was far from cool, but she had great hair. Everyone would stop what they were doing and stare at me, the cool new girl, and my life would finally be complete.

According to my ninth-grade student ID picture, I did not wear a pink-and-black-striped stretch top on the first day of school. Instead, I wore a black Ramones T-shirt, probably with seasonally appropriate Levi's jeans with added ventilation at the knees. My hair was short, but it was more Johnny Rotten than Pat Benatar—plenty cool but hardly cute. And then there were the braces, and the unfortunate truth that I did in fact look fourteen, not thirty and jaded like I always did in my fantasies.

Looking back, a black Ramones T-shirt is, in fact, cool as shit. I can show my ninth-grade ID to my grandchildren and say, "Look, kids, Granny was punk rock the first time around, when everyone was still alive and there was no Hot Topic to co-opt this shit." I can show it to the neo-mall-punks today who think that Korn is "old school" and Marilyn Manson invented fishnet way back when. Looking back, I had punk rock cred. I just didn't know it at the time. I sure wish Jimmy Stewart had dropped by and filled me in. It would have saved me a lot of misadventures. But then you wouldn't be reading this now.

In the end, for this Entrance Outfit I settle on jeans, motorcycle boots, and a plain black stretch jersey top, figuring my best bet is to be understated in the hope that they might forget how unhip I look as soon as I leave the office. Speaking of unhip, the offices of *Metal* turn out to be in a decidedly un-metal high-rise office building, and I realize as I ride up to the seventh floor in the mirrored elevator that I was probably very silly to assume that they would be above a nightclub, or maybe on the main drag of skid row in downtown Los Angeles. Heavy metal magazines are a business just like everything else, maybe not as big a business as, say, *Rolling Stone*, but in order to put out a glossy monthly and distribute it all over the country, you need secretaries and production staff and editors and circulation folks, and for all that you need office space—real office space, not vacant rooms over nightclubs, like we had for our little newsprint weeklies back home. I mentally smack myself for being so naive and step off the elevator onto the bland beige carpeting of the seventh floor.

I knock on the unmarked door of suite 721, but no one answers. I knock again and wonder if I'm being hopelessly dorky and off-the-farm for knocking and am I supposed to just walk in? After about a minute of fretting about it, I walk in, figuring what the hell. I find myself in a small room, empty but for a cheap laminate desk, on top of which sits a box of last month's issue of *Metal*. Aside from the desk, there is one lonely chair sitting in the corner, and the room looks utterly deserted. At first I take the box of magazines for a good sign, since it at least means I am in the right place, but almost immediately I realize that the lack of furniture, decor or, hello, *people* is in fact a very bad sign, and that perhaps my one possible connection has packed up and left town. I'm lamenting my bad luck when I hear voices in the back room, renewing my hope in the continued existence of my potential Lester Bangsness. I clutch my letter and make my way to the back room.

Two women, appearing to be in their mid-forties, are looking over some papers spread out on a desk in a sparsely furnished office. They're dressed business appropriately, in dark suits and heels, making me suddenly feel very stupid in my pseudo-disinterested biker-chick attire. I hold up the letter and smile weakly as they look at me like *what the fuck,* only in a polite, business-lady way.

"Um, hi, I'm a *journalist. . . .*" It sounds phony, even to me, but I press on, because really, I haven't got a choice at this point. "And, uh, Steve Peters told me that I should come by the office and maybe he would have some freelance assignments for me?" Unfortunately I don't catch myself before adding the self-conscious rise to the end of my statement, and I mentally flog myself for sounding more like Jan Brady than Lester Bangs. Way to make a first impression.

"Oh, Steve Peters." The woman behind the desk smiles sympathetically. "He doesn't work here anymore. He hasn't been here in about a month." He doesn't work here anymore? The nerve of Steve Peters, I think, abandoning me just when I need him most. Who does Steve Peters think he is? Did he not realize that I would drop everything when I got his letter, load everything I owned into my car, and drive to L.A. on the vague promise of Rikki Rocket interviews and Faster Pussycat profiles that he had dangled in front of me like a stinky mackerel? What was he thinking? I regain my composure and press on.

"Oh, gosh, that's too bad," I stutter in the understatement of the decade. If these women only knew I'd uprooted my whole life on the advice of the unsuspecting and now missing Steve Peters . . . then what? They'd probably have me put away, and they'd probably be justified. Immediately I collect myself and realize that I'm probably in the presence of the *new* editor, and that even being here in her office is probably almost as good as having gotten a letter, so I make my move. "Hey, can I give you my resume and some clips, so that you can add me to your list of available freelancers?" I'm mentally congratulating myself on my awesome save when she drops the bomb.

"Well, the reason we let Steve go is that we're going to an all-poster format, so we really don't have any need for writers. But thanks for stopping by."

Hear that noise? That whirring noise? That's Lester Bangs spinning in his fucking grave. An *all-poster format.* What is this, *Tiger Beat?* Fucking *Teen Scene?* How the hell is a *music* magazine going to an all-poster format? I hide my indignation, thank them for their time, and go back to my car, defeated and connectionless. If I were psychic, or maybe just a little more perceptive than I am, I would have seen this as the first sign of the coming apocalypse, Mach whatever. This is probably how everyone at *CREEM* felt when they saw disco coming down the pike, but at least they had each other, and I don't have four years to wait for the second coming of punk.

I should have realized right then that I had arrived in Los Angeles too late to make a difference and that I should cut my losses, turn my car around, and drive back home. But knowing when to cut my losses has never been my strong suit, so instead I drive to the nearest coffeeshop—well, not the nearest coffeeshop, but the nearest non-trendy coffeeshop, one with a giant fiberglass chicken on the roof, because even in the face of dashed dreams and missed connections, I go for the absurd. I shell out a buck-fifty for a cup of coffee, grab an *L.A. Times* and start circling classified ads, because I'm here now, damn it, and I'm going to make the best of it.

I circle five possible jobs—two typing, two temp agencies, and a bookstore. Ambitiously, I also look through the apartment ads, even though I have less than a grand left from my initial $1,500 to underwrite my *CREEM* dream, and am probably looking at about that for a deposit and first month's rent. When I finish circling all of the apartments that are under five hundred dollars a month—all six of them—I need pie. I order a piece of coconut pie and eat it joylessly, wondering, as I have repeatedly over the past few weeks, what have I gotten myself into. I have no prospects here, no backup, dwindling funds, and my one possible connection has packed up and left town. I can't afford the housing, my clothes are hopelessly unhip and unoriginal compared to everything out here, and, as if I didn't have enough to contend with in the way of morale-bashing at this point, where I was passably average looking—albeit a little nerdy—in Virginia, here in the land of leggy supermodels with suntans and silicone, I feel as though I resemble nothing so much as the Pillsbury Doughboy in metal-slut drag.

The next day, as I fill my calendar with appointments for job interviews, I tell myself that this is only temporary, I am paying my dues like any good superstar, and that soon I'll have so many freelance assignments I'll be able to leave the nine-to-five life behind and spend my mornings lying in my king-sized Dave Schools waterbed, writing up reviews of the rad shows I saw the night before.

I carry this cocksure attitude with me to my first interview, where, fortunately for me, the tie guy who interviews me is starry-eyed over my rock 'n' roll cred as listed on my resume.

"Wow. Says here you interviewed Henry Rollins," he says, his wide eyes belying his attempted corporate nonchalance. I am momentarily taken aback; with his starchy attire and junior-executive haircut, he strikes me as the last person who'd be impressed with Henry Rollins. "What was that like?"

"He was pretty cool," I say blithely, not letting on that not only was I scared shitless but I had taken my high school squatter-punk boyfriend Andy along and let him ask all the questions while I sat on a speaker, chewing my lip and fiddling with my tape recorder. I wrote the article and I got the byline (though I was honest enough to share it with Andy), but my contribution to the whole experience consisted mostly of sitting dumbstruck and staring at Henry in his little nylon shorts. That and turning beet red when he turned to me and said in his best serial killer voice, "You know, I'm not getting *laid* enough on this tour," which I think was a calculated attempt to fluster me, and I definitely cooperated. Not with the lack of sex, but the flustering. I think I may have even *squeaked*. But Tie Guy doesn't need to know that. "It was the cover story," I shrug.

"You interview anybody else I might have heard of?" Tie Guy is starting to lose his starchy edge and is actually leaning across his desk, eager for tales of punk rock insider dirt. Not exactly what I'd expect from a guy who looks more Boy Scout than Black Flag, but I'm one to talk. Not wanting to let him down, I fish around for another recognizable name to drop.

"Actually I just asked Glenn Danzig a few questions last week after his show in Tucson," I say as casually as I can muster, figuring my true role as mistaken-identity bimbo can be my little secret for now.

"No way—the Misfits *rock*!"

It is at this point that I realize I have the job. We make some small talk about my editing skills and experience with WordPerfect (none at all, but who's telling), then he offers

me the job and I accept. Just like that—thanks, Aunt Delta.
This ain't no Mudd Club, but it's rent money and the boss
digs the Misfits. For ten dollars an hour, I am now a full-
time editor of workers' compensation claims. Rock on!

With the forthcoming money from my shiny new day job
and *L.A. Times* classifieds in hand, my West Coast mom and
I go looking for an apartment for me. I say no to an
adorable efficiency bungalow in West Hollywood—one,
because it backs up to the freeway, and two, because it has
easily accessible ground-floor windows, something that has
to be pointed out to this naive southern girl. Sometimes
loco parentis is a handy thing. After rejecting three build-
ings that are so seedy we don't even get out of the car, I
sign a lease on an efficiency apartment on Normandie
Avenue right off Hollywood Boulevard. The mottled brown
shag carpeting looks like the jungle room rug up and died,
but for $395 a month, it's my kind of place. Besides, it has
a Murphy bed, an ironing board that pops out of the wall,
and a dresser built into the closet, which places it way
ahead of any also-rans in sheer weirdness points. We don't
have Murphy beds in Virginia; in fact, we barely have efficiency apartments. I feel incredibly cosmopolitan as I dine
on my first take-out burrito from the corner taco stand in
my new digs. In addition to the Murphy bed, I have a folding card table, a single wooden chair from the Salvation
Army, and a sickly little plant I found by the trashcans. I
feel like I'm playing house, but at the same time I'm a wee

bit smug about my spartan surroundings. It's not much, but it's all mine, and I did it without having to resort to financial help or even loans from my parents, a fact that I am quick to point out during my victorious first phone call home on my very own phone. "Yes, I have a job, and I have an apartment, and guess what, I even *bought a can of peas!*" With my electric typewriter and my coffeemaker perking away, I feel like Kerouac, or Hemingway, needing only the bare essentials because the rest is for pansies.

Q: *Did you really just compare yourself to Kerouac and Hemingway?*

A: *Not technically. If you read between the lines, I was actually comparing my* furniture *to theirs, which is much less pretentious.*

My neighborhood is not particularly glamorous, either. I'm on the eastern edge of Hollywood, which I'll soon come to learn is the less desirable edge. West Hollywood is trendy, pricy, and, well, *gay.* East Hollywood is mostly poor immigrants—Mexicans, Central Americans, and, inexplicably, Armenians. The souvenir shops and tour offices don't extend down to my end of Hollywood Boulevard; instead I have liquor stores, massage parlors, and rooms by the week. Around the corner from my apartment, a low-rent strip mall is home to an even lower-rent strip club, the intriguingly named Jumbo's Clown Room. I'm told—though I don't investigate it myself—that the "Jumbo" in the club's name could be appropriately applied to some of their dancers, many of whom are too fat, too old, or too strung out to dance at the upscale clubs at the other end of Hollywood. The only business that I patronize in my neighborhood is Mister Kim's, on the corner of my street, where Mister Kim always saves me a newspaper and the beer is extra cold.

Q: *Why do I feel like I've heard of Jumbo's Clown Room?*

A: *Maybe because Courtney Love danced there in the eighties, in her pre-Kurt, pre-plastic surgery, pre-IV-diet days. Also, from what I understand, Jumbo's is now a hipster burlesque hangout and boasts the best-looking dancers in Hollywood. I'm not exactly sure how I feel about that.*

Even though, like my neighborhood, it's far from hip, I dig my new job from the start. I have my own upholstery-covered cubicle and a computer—my own desk, even, with a little metal plaque that has my name on it! I tack up a picture of Suzi Quatro and one of Keith Richards and claim my cubicle as my own. I don't feel the least bit demoralized or insulted by the concept of the cube farm; I am basically just happy that there are no hams waiting to be gift-wrapped. Andrew, the guy who hired me, is neck and neck with me for obscure music references dropped into daily conversation, and my fellow editors are a good-naturedly disgruntled bunch of would-be novelists, screenwriters, musicians, and poets, which means snappy patter is mandatory. Our file assistant, a six-foot-two punkabilly teenager in a zoot suit and pompadour, keeps me up to speed on upcoming shows and cool places to shop in Hollywood between cigarette breaks and impromptu manic dances. Then, as if I hadn't lucked out enough, there are the reports I'm being paid to edit.

The claims we deal with are all job-stress-related or, as our billboards say, *el estres de trabajo*. Most of our clients speak Spanish, which means most of the reports I edit have either been through a translator or were filled out by someone whose English leaves something to be desired. Sometimes both. In any case, the reports border on dadaism a lot of the time, and Andrew and I devote far too many of our working hours archiving the "greatest quotes file," which includes gems like "I was very popular at work because of my earring but then my boss was yelling at me all the time, the bitch whore" and "I was eating cereal in the break room and the boss grabbed my bowl and threw it away, saying that cereal was a food to be eaten at home and not at work."

Q: *That's very cruel of you to make fun of these poor people who suffer from job stress.*

A: *In the case of our employer, "suffering" is a relative term. According to California law at the time, if you could prove that 10 percent of the stress in your life was caused by your job, you qualified for workers' compensation.*

Q: *Ten percent? Is there anybody whose job doesn't cause 10 percent of their stress?*

A: *Exactly. My employer went on to singlehandedly almost bankrupt the California Workers' Compensation system and greatly* *influence the sweeping California Workers' Compensation Reform Act of 1993—but it sure was fun while it lasted.*

I'm having so much fun hitting taquerias and swap meets with my new work friends that I sometimes have to remind myself of my real purpose in Los Angeles. After a full day of editing and writing, the temptation to go out drinking at a piano bar with the guys from work is great—but you don't achieve rock 'n' roll greatness in a piano bar. It's easy to get comfortable, though, with a group of people who don't expect you to impress them with your nonexistent rock 'n' roll hipness, and I really do like just about everyone at my office. I don't even mind that Andrew's standard nonwork uniform is the dreaded paisley shirt. It's not what I came to L.A. for, though, and after a laid-back month of Trivial Pursuit parties in the Valley and sushi nights with the girls, I know I need to get back to my main objective. I hole up in my apartment for a weekend, combing the local music magazines for opportunities, soon getting my name added to the freelancing rosters of free weeklies *Rock City News* and *Hollywood Rocks.* Getting on the list is a heck of a lot easier than I ever thought it would be; the fact that I even own a typewriter and plan to use it has one editor practically fellating me on the spot. When pressed, he admits that most of their submissions are handwritten on torn-out notebook paper. My English degree and years of published work are just the icing on the cake; apparently it's the little things, like being able to form complete sentences and come reasonably close to meeting a deadline that qualify you for this work. Of course, it would be tough for them to be too choosy considering the pay. Like the free weeklies at home, they don't pay anything other than comp admittance at shows and the occasional last-choice swag thrown my way, but the journey of a thousand miles starts with a single motorcycle-booted step, and I am stepping. I review Rude Awakening, a band from, of all places, Richmond, and earn my first Hollywood byline less than a month after my arrival. I feel vindicated, proudly sending copies of my review home to my parents to show them that their fears were obviously for nothing as I am on my way now.

My first couple of months writing for the weeklies are heady. My name is on the guest list at the Whisky, the Roxy, and the Troubador, places I've read about for years in *CREEM* and the other magazines I slavishly pored over. The fact that my reviews arrive on time and with all of the words spelled correctly keep the editors calling, and I even get sent to review a couple of fairly big name groups—that is, if Night Ranger can still be considered a big name in 1990. I feel like all of that time I spent the summer after graduation sending out resumes and clips is finally amounting to something, even if the something is not exactly a direct result of my mailings. If I hadn't been so relentless with the query letters, I never would have gotten that one fateful response from Steve Peters, and then I never would have packed up and moved to L.A., where I discovered the promising world of free weeklies just waiting for me to show up and take them by storm. I feel I am finally where I am supposed to be. Things are happening. I am making a name for myself.

With Night Ranger being as far as I've made it up the journalistic food chain, I don't have a chance of scoring a guest list spot for the Iggy Pop show at the Hollywood Palladium. I missed out on Iggy Pop at the Richmond Mosque in 1981 because I was only fourteen and didn't have a good enough fake ID to get in. I eventually did get my chance to see him live; unfortunately, it was at William and Mary Hall six years later, and some dumbass frat-boy loser—probably one of the same ones who yelled "weirdo chick" at me from the windows of Fraternity Row—hit Iggy in the face with half a grapefruit hurled from the stands and pissed him off. This was the tour where Iggy was opening for the Pretenders. That, and the fact that it was at William and Mary—*hello*—made it cold consolation for the show I missed, which culminated in a riot replete with police brutality and bloodshed, just like any good punk rock show. The grapefruit would not have been out of place in Richmond; nor would it have been out of place at any number of Stooges shows in the seventies, where Iggy would have hurled back at least a few choice words as a rejoinder. But this is 1987 Iggy, a kinder, gentler Iggy, who just wants to put on a show and isn't serving anything harder than root beer backstage (yeah, I know because I was there, Bucky). Iggy at the Palladium promises to be true punk rock. I will be there.

Q: *Did you say Iggy Pop was opening for the Pretenders? Didn't you mean that the other way around?*

A: *Would that I did. It calls to mind the 1967 tour that had*

*Jimi Hendrix opening for the Monkees—which is exactly what
I said in my review of it in the William and Mary student paper,
or tried to, but my review was rejected by the sorority-girl editor
for being "too unobjective," which isn't even a word, Miss Editor-
Britches.*

The night of the Iggy Pop show, I don my Sun Records
shirt, now slightly worn in thanks to the rough machinery
of the apartment laundry machines, and drive myself down
to the Hollywood Palladium. Even though as the new kid in
town I won't be covering the show for any papers and
indeed will have to pay for my own ticket, just the fact that
I am on the rosters now makes me walk a little taller. I'm
not just "Anne from Virginia" anymore, I'm "Anne from
Rock City News," just in case anybody's asking, and that's
enough to keep my shoulders straight as I cough up the ten
bucks for my ticket and make my way to the floor. There
are a couple of opening bands, Celebrity Skin and Alice in
Chains, neither of which I know from Adam's housecat,
but because it's Iggy, I want to get there early and get a
good spot. I wind my way through the crowd, between
elbows and shoulders, using my usual under-the-radar
small-person technique. I notice that I am seeing more and
more elbows and fewer and fewer shoulders as I make my
way to the middle of the crowd. I am by far the smallest
person I can see. I am also the only female. I wonder what
the deal is—do L.A. girls not like Iggy Pop? How could
they not? How could anyone not? I grit my teeth as I plant
my feet and stake out my spot, waiting for Iggy to start.

I actually kind of like Celebrity Skin—what I can see of them, anyway. They've got a New York Dolls thing going on that I can respect, some makeup, some costumes, and even some dancing girls.

Q: *Dancing girls?*

A: *Yes, dancing girls make everything better. There's not a band alive that couldn't benefit from a dancing girl or two.*

I dig Celebrity Skin. I can't say the same for Alice in Chains. Cool name—you'd think they'd give you a show with that, but no, they come out in flannel and sweat-pants—*sweatpants*—and act like they're doing us a favor by making us wait another half an hour for Iggy Pop. *Losers!*

Q: *I guess they showed you, huh?*

A: *If by "showing me" you mean that they showed me that it's possible to get rich and famous without putting any effort into your stage show and then blow it all through drug addiction and self-indulgence and end up dying alone and miserable and have no one find your body for weeks, then, yeah, they sure showed me. Hey, I know it's harsh, folks, but these are the facts. I just report 'em. Little did we know that within months we wouldn't be able to dig our way out of smug Seattle junkies in flannel. Had I known at the time, I would have done something drastic to try and save rock 'n' roll, and maybe Layne Staley's life in the bargain. My kingdom for a can of Aqua-Net!*

As it is, I take no greater action than withholding my applause. Not that they care. As far as Alice in Chains are concerned, we are intruding on a very private moment and they'd just as soon we all go home. If it weren't for the promise of Iggy Pop, I surely would. But I've been promised the Godfather of Punk, damn it, the one forgotten boy, whose lyrics Melissa and I cranked up in eighth grade while we dolled ourselves up in fishnets and glitter to go stand outside clubs we couldn't even pretend we had a chance of getting into. I was there to see the poet whose positively foul version of "Louie Louie" made my mother threaten to tear the tone arm off my Emerson portable record player. For Iggy, I'd wait through Celine Dion *and* Alice in Chains. Finally, Iggy takes the stage—and the crowd goes wild.

Q: *God, that's such a cliché.*

A: *No, I am totally serious. The crowd really did go wild. And not in a good way.*

To say Iggy's appearance caused a shift in the crowd dynamic would be a gross understatement along the lines of saying my father would rather I had stayed in Richmond. There is a sudden lurching, in waves, forward and back, interspersed with bursts of directionless activity, almost like small explosions throughout the crowd. I can't tell what song Iggy is singing. I can't tell much of anything about what is going on around me at that time outside of my immediate surroundings. From my spot in the dead center of the floor, I can't see anything but T-shirted chests and backs, smashing up against my face, depriving me of air until I think I am going to pass out, then backing up and smashing again. Every time the crowd lurches, I have to run, holding on to whoever and whatever is closest, to keep from falling. My feet sometimes leave the floor entirely and I just ride with the crowd. At first I am panicked because I know there is no way I'll be able to keep this up for the length of the show. Eventually I'll let my guard down, or get exhausted, and I'll fall. Then what? *Then I'll die*, I think, and am suddenly filled with a feeling of peace, probably magnified by lack of oxygen to the brain. But really, I will die—and what better way to go then smashed to death at an Iggy Pop concert at the Hollywood Palladium? As endings go, it is nothing if not rock 'n' roll. I'll be a martyr. It will be great. And I will die wearing a Sun Records shirt and motorcycle boots, and when I get to heaven, Lester Bangs and Darby Crash will say, "Hey, cool chick, come have a celestial beer with us!" Even as I decide that I am OK with my fate, I can feel myself going limp against the crush of bodies.

"DON'T FALL DOWN!" Not a message from above, but from behind. Even over the din of the crowd, I hear it shouted, more than once, and I instinctively know that it's meant for me. Almost as if I sent out a silent alarm the second I gave up, somehow, the cavalry is on the way. I hear the voice shouting again, this time closer, right behind me.

"DON'T FALL," the voice commands. I feel a tug on my back belt loop and realize someone's hooked his fingers through it. I do my best to stay standing with each wave, and every time the crowd moves, the voice shouts again,

"STAY UP STAY UP STAY UP!" as we go careening together, forward and back. There's a pause in the music, a break between songs, and the crowd stops surging and waits for the next command. A thick arm wraps around my waist and suddenly, wordlessly, I am dragged backward through the crowd. The drums start up again just as we reach the back edge of the crowd, and my anonymous savior tosses me out of harm's way with one forceful swing, disappearing back into the crowd before I even get a look at his face.

Q: *So did you ever get to thank him?*

A: *No, I never saw him again. Whoever you are, guy, I owe you big time. Being a rock 'n' roll martyr would have been cool on paper, but the reality of being trampled into martyrdom by a mob probably would have hurt a lot, not to mention that martyrdom is inherently fatal. So thanks, dude. You are my rock 'n' roll superhero.*

I don't remember anything after I was pulled out of the crowd. I couldn't even tell you a single song that Iggy did. But you know what? I'd have to say that was probably one of the most punk-rock moments of my entire life. Good on ya, Iggy. You almost killed me, but you missed again, so you're gonna have to keep trying next week.

After the Iggy show, I lay low for a couple of weeks. A brush with death has a tendency to make you want to avoid crowds,

reflect, watch *Lucy,* and eat Pop Tarts. You know, enjoy the little things. Until one night, close to eleven, I'm in Von's
Supermarket, shopping in the produce section. I've stopped
by for a single girl's supper of Kraft macaroni and cheese and
strawberries. It's a balanced diet, don'cha know, equal parts
boxed and fresh. I'm shuffling through the cartons of strawberries, looking for the plumpest ones, when I see a familiar,
if entirely incongruous figure, all in black, fondling the can-
taloupes on the other side of the bin. My mind is so blown by
the juxtaposition that I can't believe I'm really seeing who I
think I'm seeing. I wait to get a glimpse of an identifiable tattoo so that I can make a positive ID before I say anything. He
reaches out for a 'lope, and yep, there it is in all its boo-
spooky glory, the horned skull poking out from beneath the
sleeve of his T-shirt.

"Glenn Danzig?"

"Oh, hey!" Danzig's voice is a little hoarse, tired
maybe—it is late—and confused, like he thinks he should
know me somehow.

"Anne Soffee. I met you a couple of months ago in Tucson." Probably a common occurrence for him, what with him
being a rock star and all, girls coming up and reminding you
that they met you here or there. To his credit, he gallantly
pretends to remember me.

"Oh yeah, Tucson. Good to see you," he says, then indi-
cates the basket hanging from his massive forearm. "Just doin'
a little shopping."

"Yeah, me too," I say, picking up the closest carton of
strawberries and holding them up—see, I'm shopping—and
grinning like an idiot. There is an awkward beat, or maybe

five, and I feel my face turning as red as the strawberries in my hand. "Well, take it easy," I cry jauntily and turn and run smack into an oncoming cart. Maybe he didn't see me.

"Yeah, you too, and watch where you're going," he advises. Shit.

Q: *Wow, you're a real klutz, huh?*

A: *I don't know how I manage, but somehow I only ever trot out my most embarrassing, klutzy maneuvers in front of rock stars. Case in point: I have gotten toilet paper stuck to my heel exactly once in my life. It was backstage at a Robert Plant concert. See what I mean?*

Adding insult to idiocy, when I get home, I notice that the strawberries I grabbed in my haste to appear nonchalant are moldy on the bottom. But it's all good. I may be a clumsy nerd with moldy strawberries for dessert, but I am still living a life where I run into Glenn Danzig in the produce section on a Tuesday night. And that's really all I ever asked for.

✟

Another night, another piano bar. I realize I am getting too complacent with my scant assignments from the free week-lies, spending too much time with my work friends and not enough time trolling seedy bars for hair gods about whom I can weave wry articles in glossy magazines. I resolve to find more work, and arm myself with a stack of music papers and a highlighter pen, searching for the job that will Make Me Famous.

Unfortunately for my champagne dreams, the majority of the want ads in the music papers seem to be for unpaid internships. Record labels, production companies, recording studios, and talent agencies all seem eager to exploit the dreams of the young and resume-less. I respond to an ad, one of the few that mention editing skills, and get a call from Cyndi Walton, a writer looking for someone to transcribe her interview tapes for publication. To make sure we are all straight on how this works: she meets the rock star, shoots the breeze with said rock star for a while, probably collects swag from said rock star, perhaps a backstage pass to see said rock star perform, then the unpaid intern—who could be me, if I play my cards right—spends hours typing up the conversation that they had, for which Cyndi will get the byline, the paycheck, and the chance to hang out with more rock stars.

Where do I sign up? She gives me an address to which I am supposed to report on Saturday morning. I consult my Thomas Guide and find out that she lives two blocks from me, behind the Adobe Liquor store. Come Saturday, I fortify myself with black coffee and walk the two blocks to Cyndi's building. She buzzes me in and meets me in the stairwell in jeans, glasses, and a ponytail. I feel like I am seeing behind the wizard's curtain—this is a real rock journalist? She looks just like me. I follow her up to her apartment, wondering if I am being duped, wondering what really constitutes being duped in a situation like this. I mean, I've never heard of her, but that doesn't mean she doesn't write for *something*, somewhere. Either way, I'm working for nothing, so what's the difference? Either she's a legitimate journalist or she's some chick getting free typing. I'm doing the same thing no matter what her credentials are or are not.

Her apartment is an efficiency, like mine only without the Murphy bed. She shows me to a desk with a computer—which points to her possibly being legit, because, hey, I'm a nerd and even I don't have my own computer at home—and a tape recorder and hands me a stack of tapes. The first one is an interview with Lemmy of Motörhead. I am momentarily heartened; at least she has however much cred it would take to get an interview with Lemmy. It's not until later that I find out that all it takes to get an audience with Lemmy are two X chromosomes and a willingness to display a couple of the attributes to which they contribute. I get comfortable at the desk and start typing.

The interview is OK, kind of dry. You could probably take this conversation, I figure, and jazz it up with a lot of off-the-wall side notes and bizarre unrelated outside stuff like the writers at *CREEM* used to do and then it might be fun to read. That or cut it down by about 70 percent and only leave the gossip and double entendres, of which there are several, Lemmy being Lemmy and all. As it is, though, it reads like a technical manual. It's about as much fun as those interviews where they spend three pages talking about what kinds of guitar strings they use, only not as informative. Cyndi offers me a cup of coffee, and I accept graciously.

"So, what do you do with this after I type it?"

She looks at me blankly. "What do you mean, what do I do with it?"

"I mean, are you going to use this as the basis for an article? Are you planning to, like, take out the best quotes and use them? Or maybe add some history?"

She frowns. "No, I really hadn't considered that. I usually just submit them as Q-and-A interviews, just typed up like they are." She looks at me hopefully and adds, "Of course, if you're interested in writing it up as an article, that would be great."

"Would I get a byline?"

The frown returns. "No, I can't really give an intern a byline. But it would look good for you when it comes to future projects."

Future projects. Does she mean future projects with money and a byline, or future projects like the one I am working on now? I'm reminded of my friend Sam's dilemma when he started saving up for a car in high school. His father told him that maybe if he praised the Lord a little bit more—"in, addition, of course, to all the praising that I already do," Sam had reported dryly—he might get that car that he wanted sooner. Sam couldn't figure out if his dad meant *he'd* pay for the car or the Lord would, and subsequently had no idea whether any additional Lord-praising would be worth his while.

After a few more questions and answers with Cyndi that are about as dry as the ones she shared with Lemmy, I realize that I have about as much chance of getting a byline out of this gig as Sam did getting a Ford Mustang from Jesus. I thank her for the opportunity to do her typing and let her know that she won't be seeing me again, no hard feelings. I'm willing to do the intern thing, it's not that I'm too proud to pay my dues . . . I'd just prefer to pay them to someone who ranks a little higher than me on the rock 'n' roll food chain. Because otherwise, I can stay at home and do my own typing and get just as far.

And besides, I make better coffee.

✠

Saturday afternoon, my third month in Los Angeles. I've been out shopping on Melrose Avenue and I'm on my way home, empty-handed and depressed. It seems like everyone in Hollywood is tall, tan, and lean, with even, perfect features and straight white teeth. On the same wavelength as the heavy metal bands who come to Hollywood to hit it big, in Hollywood one also finds the pretty girls who do the same. You guessed it, the prettiest girl from every city in America, right here in my new hometown. It is all kinds of unfair, too, because the ones who don't have big breasts can buy them on the open market once they get here, which means that my one ace-in-the-hole physical attribute isn't even anything special in Hollywood. *Everyone* here has at least a D cup. On the bright side, it is a lot easier for me to find a bra that fits here than it is in Richmond, where the pert-breasted shopgirls always just shake their heads sympathetically at me when I tell them my size, then lead me to something flesh-toned and monstrous with fifteen hooks in the back.

Under the best circumstances, I'm not a good shopper. I am too picky and set in my ways. I go shopping in desperation because I have no pants, or shoes, and I come back with another stretchy black top to cram in my built-in dresser drawer that is already overfull of stretchy black tops. Or I optimistically buy something totally out of character, like a brightly patterned jacket or a pair of fitted pants made of nubby silk, and then my new purchase migrates to the back of my closet while I continue to rotate the same assortment of blue jeans and stretchy black tops. At least in heavy metal Hollywood, I have a greater assortment of stretchy black tops from which to choose—velvet, lace, long-sleeved, off the shoulder, even stretchy black tops with tiny skeletons or daggers, even one with the word *fuck* woven into the fabric. Richmond isn't big on stretchy black tops, and certainly not ones with skeletons and daggers on them. As my Methodist Nana would say, "It just doesn't suit," not like a pastel twin set would, anyway. I can only imagine how much the *fuck* top wouldn't suit. Talbot's isn't keen on the stretchy black tops, but Retail Slut on Melrose has a plenty of 'em. I would have bought some, too, but I got all down and discouraged when I realized I was probably the only one in the shop who had not been in a Mötley Crüe video and I left empty-handed.

I'm heading back up Hollywood Boulevard, close to my apartment, when I realize—or think I realize—that there is no one driving the car in front of me. It's a gorgeous red fastback Mustang, completely restored and growling like a tiger, but as far as I can tell it seems to be careening down Hollywood Boulevard of its own free will. It occurs to me that maybe I've stumbled on a movie being filmed, as I've already done several times since my arrival, or that maybe a small child has stolen the car and is on a joyride. A conscientious citizen to the core, I whip my Hyundai into the left lane and pull up next to the Mustang at the next light. I peer into the driver's side window and see, not a child, not Hollywood movie magic, but Glenn Danzig in black wraparound sunglasses, his head not quite reaching the top of the leather headrest. I toot the horn at him. I am a shameless nerd, I admit it. He waves warily, probably thinking *Jesus Christ, it's the freaky chick from the Von's; she must be stalking me.* I wave back, pleased as punch, realizing that odds are Glenn Danzig probably lives in my neighborhood. For joy! The lack of a new stretchy black top seems entirely inconsequential to me now. I go home, put on "Twist of Cain" and bask in the new cachet that my dingy one-room apartment has been granted by the proximity of a true-to-life—albeit diminutive—rock star.

Q: *Now that you seem to be running into Glenn Danzig everywhere but in the bathtub, does it ever occur to you to ask him for an interview that you can maybe then sell to an actual paying magazine?*

A: *The official answer: There is an unspoken understanding when you live in Los Angeles that you don't accost celebrities in their daily lives and ask them to read your script, listen to your demo, or grant you an interview, no matter how much it might help your budding career. They're people too, and they've got enough hassles without being solicited by the strawberries. The real answer: No, I was always too nervous.*

The next month, because I just don't learn, I respond to another classified ad in *Hollywood Rocks*, this one for a publicity intern. I figure publicity and journalism aren't too far apart and I'm sure I can write a better press release than the competition, so I give it a shot. I send them my resume and a puffed-up cover letter referring to some punk rock shows I may or may not have helped promote back in Richmond and sit back and wait. Sure enough, I get a call asking me to come in for an interview the next week.

This time, I play it safe and wear business attire—not that I had much choice, as the interview is on my lunch break. Already I have a better feeling about this internship, just on the basis of their having an actual office and keeping business hours. Signs point to this being somebody's real job. Not mine, but somebody's, which is at least a step up from the Motörhead tape experience. I have the address written on a Post-it note, and I check numbers along Hollywood Boulevard until I find it. Checking the cross street, I see that the office is on the corner of Hollywood and Vine—holy cliché, Batman! I can't wait to tell my parents. There are so few things about my new life that they understand. Last week I had frantically called home to tell my mother that we had just seconds ago had an earthquake— my first earthquake!

"Where are you?" she asked breathlessly.

"I'm at the 7-Eleven." I had been buying a newspaper and a package of Twizzlers when the quake happened, shaking the pork rinds off their racks.

"Is that where they tell you to go in case of an earthquake?" She tries to understand. She really does. I'm sure she knows Hollywood and Vine, though, so I make a mental note to call her.

The building itself is musty and regal, Deco-era architecture complete with grated elevators. I ride the snail-paced cage up to the tenth floor, simultaneously praying that I actually make it alive and wondering how on God's green earth a heavy metal publicity firm ended up in this film noir building. When I reach ten, prayers answered, I drag the gate open with all my might—at least one thing in the building is heavy metal—and start checking doors. Most of the offices have cryptic plaques—"Simms and Hutton LLC," "Vista Enterprises Inc.," and the intriguing "Shangri La." The last door on the left has an equally vague name—Around the World Incorporated—but the picture painted on the frosted-glass window tells me this must be the place. A globe floats in the center of the door with vague representations of the continents, sort of, on its face. Curving around each side of the globe is an arm. The arm on the right side wears a business suit and cuff links, the arm on the left a zippered leather jacket, chain bracelet, and skull ring. The two hands meet in a hearty handshake in front of the globe, just below a star-shaped blob that may or may not be Australia.

"Hi, you must be Anne," a voice calls from behind the partially opened door. "Come on in and we'll be right with you."

I step into the office and immediately approve. This is what I had expected *Metal*'s office to be like when I first arrived. The walls are covered with framed pictures of shirtless, pouting musicians and the desks are piled with swag—stickers, CDs, T-shirts, and glossy photos. Three young women in various permutations of video-babe attire are hustling around, stuffing manila envelopes with papers pulled from a row of piles, and, in the corner, a Keith Richards clone is propped up on a tatty waiting room chair in full-on junkie nod.

"I'm Morgan," says the babe who called me in, a tiny elf with a huge mane of dark hair and tight leather pants. "Nice to meet you. This is Heather . . ." she points to a redhead in a spandex dress. "She's my business partner, and that's Renee, our other intern." *Other* intern . . . sounds good, like maybe they've already hired me—insomuch as I can be hired to work for free, I mean. I wave at the other intern, a sullen, bony blonde in acid-washed jeans and an off-the-shoulder lace top who looks to be about eighteen. "And that's Danny," she says, pointing to the nodder. "He's our graphic artist. He painted the door." Aha. I glance at the photos on the walls, seeing a few names I recognize— Little Caesar, Vinnie Vincent Invasion, well, OK, two names I recognize (as long as no one asks me to name any of their songs). I see a lot of other bands I don't recognize, all cut from the same cloth, no doubt the hottest bands in whatever towns they were in before they came here.

"So let's talk a little bit about what you'll be doing here." Hot damn, I *am* already hired. Morgan walks me around the three-room office and points to different piles of papers. "What we do for our talent is get a buzz going. We take their press pack and their CD and we send it to press and then we follow up." She picks up a thick stapled packet of papers that look as if they've been photocopied a million times and hands it to me. "These are magazines around the country. This is the master list that we use for our mailings. What we need you to do is call all these magazines and make sure they're still in business and the addresses are still good." My thrill falters, just a little. I'm OK, though, I can do this.

"Right," I say, taking the list from her. "And what else would I be doing, you know, as an intern—for instance, once I finish this?" I try and sound capable, like I will be finished in no time. Maybe then they'll let me write some press releases, or even a band bio or two.

"Well," says Morgan thoughtfully, looking around the room. "I suppose you could assist Renee while she fills those envelopes." Assist Renee. The other intern. That would make me the *assistant* intern. Three thousand miles, four years in college, five years of published writing and here is my pot of gold—an unpaid position as an assistant intern. As Iggy himself said, "I never thought it'd come to this, baby."

"Will there be any writing duties on this job?" I ask brazenly, more out of frustration than any real balls. I can feel my cheeks flushing from the indignity of being appointed assistant to a teenage intern. "I do have an English degree, and a lot of experience publishing my—"

"Oh, of *course,* Anne," Morgan squeaks way too cheerily, hustling me into her office and closing the door, her huge white smile moving chummily close to my ear. "I didn't want to say anything, you know, in front of Renee, but with your *credentials*, we hope to have you doing *press* with our talent as soon as you get to know the ropes. And you know," here she leans in even closer, her huge mane of hair closing in around my face, "Heather and I have done so many tours that we are just *over* them, you know, and so the next time one of our bands *tours*, well, that's something else that we would need a *skilled* person to do."

Tour. With a band! Visions of laminated all-access passes dance in my head. I am calling up newspapers and crossing off names before Morgan is even out of the room. Were my brain not so clouded by dreams of a gypsy life on the road with a busload of hair gods, it might have occurred to me to ask when the last time was that they had represented a touring band. Were I not dizzy with the notion of leaning up against the Marshall stacks and watching Little Caesar play whatever song it is they play in Omaha, Nebraska, I might have compared notes with Renee about how long she'd been there and what she'd been promised. And were I not already mentally packing my bags for my first European tour with the Vinnie Vincent Invasion, I might have even thought to get something— anything—in writing. But this is rock 'n' roll, and I am still green enough to be easily snowed by little big-haired women in leather pants. I spend my whole lunch break making phone calls and promise to come back and do it again the next day. For my art I will suffer, and for a chance to ride the bus, I will starve. Besides, it looks like I might need to think about fitting into some appropriately small leather pants to work here, so I better start skipping some lunches anyway. As I dial the *Topeka Capital Journal,* I feel as though I have taken another little jump on the continuum from gift-ham wrapper to the new millennium's answer to Lester Bangs. *Viva le rock 'n' roll.*

4

Payola Means Never Having to Say "You Suck"
Where Everybody Knows Your Name Except for the Girl in the Leather Bra

by my six-month anniversary in Los Angeles, my schedule is so full I barely have time to be homesick anymore. Between writing reviews for three different weeklies, stuffing envelopes and making follow-up calls at Around the World, and continuing to hopefully send clips and resumes to "legit" magazines, I am starting to feel like a real writer. Of course, I'd feel *more* real if just one of my writing jobs was a paying one, but that's neither here nor there. I've dropped almost ten pounds with the help of Weight Watchers and their decidedly un-rock 'n' roll rah-rah meetings. My motivation is not the cheesy blue ribbon or the even cheesier grandma-issue lapel pin but the promise of slinky leather slutwear with which to drape my shrinking form. My day job is still going strong at this point, so I do not want for rent money, beer money, or companions with whom I can hone my biting one-liners in the white patent leather booths at the Dresden Room after work. Unfortunately, those very one-liners are starting to cause problems for me with my editors at the weekly, who apparently were never fans of *CREEM*, Lester Bangs, or the biting one-liner in general, which is my literary stock in trade.

The first sign of trouble comes when Terri Ann, my editor at *Screamer*, sends me to the Roxy to review Wikked Gypsy, a local band with a big marketing budget. They're part of the fanfaronade of L.A. Guns/Guns N' Roses wannabe bands infesting the strip, all black shag and piercings and glam junkie posing. I suffer through their comically bad performance and then gleefully dash off what is, to me, a review worthy of Boy Howdy that is every bit as silly as Wikked Gypsy itself.

Wikked Gypsy

at the Roxy

by Anne Thomas Soffee

When I entered the Roxy for my first-ever Wikked Gypsy show, I was confronted with a throng of what appeared to be adoring Wikked Gypsy fans. It seemed that every other person in the club was wearing a T-shirt emblazoned with the slogan "It's a Sikk World," presumably in homage to the dyslexic rock 'n' rollers.

"Wow," I thought. "Such a following these guys have! Why haven't I heard of them before?" Mentally kicking myself for being so late to discover this obvious Next Big Thing, I made my way to the bar to purchase a golden beverage. There, strategically positioned beside the tap, was Wikked Gypsy's manager, handing out free T-shirts (poor spelling as a marketing tool— +10 goofy points) to anyone within reach.

I collected my free shirt and went in to hear their set. On seeing guitarist Ash's raggy clothing,

I wondered why the manager didn't give him a free shirt—until I realized that he had intentionally ripped out the upper left quarter of his shirt so that we might admire his nipple ring (gratuitous body piercing—+ 5 goofy points). We were all duly impressed.

Good thing, too, because Wikked Gypsy didn't do much else to impress us all night. Their playing was decent, and their writing was OK, in a clichéd Hollywood-sleaze kinda way, but somehow I expected more, given the hype and money that someone is obviously pouring into these guys.

Still searching for some redeeming feature, I turned my attention to lead singer Stef (guy attempting to be studly while sporting girl's name—+10 goofy points). From his shades to his plentiful jewelry to his long, straight, middle-parted hair, Stef was a ringer for Ian Astbury (imitating someone not worth imitating— +15 goofy points). Like the band's playing, his singing was OK, sure, but sadly lacking in any real substance or individuality. Oh, and in case you hadn't noticed the pattern, rounding out the lineup were Jos on bass and PJ on drums (no one in the band has a last name—+ a big 50 goofy points).

Meanwhile, over on stage left, a scene worthy of Spiñal Tap was taking place. Ash wanted out of his Steven Tyler–style scarf, but couldn't figure out the knot, but even with a show this ludicrous, the show must go on, so a lackey had taken the stage to work on it while Ash played (roadie utilized for grooming purposes—+20 goofy points).

With any other band, such preening would have
been distracting, but with Wikked Gypsy, there was
nothing to be distracted from—not musically, anyway.
Their songs blurred into one long Sunset Strip drone,
the same L.A. glam/trash/thrash that we've all heard
too many times before. The only standout was "Emotion Number One (Cry)," a slow, Zeppelin-style ballad
that Stef dedicated to a friend. It seemed to have all the
soul that was missing from the rest of the set, which
made Wikked Gypsy all the more frustrating—they
obviously have the ability to write and perform interesting, original material, so why don't they do it? Are
they too busy coordinating their nipple rings to their
scarves? If that's the case, they'd better get used to
reviews that pay more attention to their looks than to
their music. Hey, guys, it's only fair.

To say I am proud of my review would be putting it mildly.
I naively believe that this review will somehow be spotted
by a music-loving benefactor who, like me, laments the
rock journalism days of yore and has long harbored a
dream to resurrect *CREEM* from the ashes. He'll call
Screamer and beg Terri Ann for my contact info, because he
will immediately see that I am a kindred spirit, a Lester
Bangs in the making, and he'll hire me on as a staff writer,
where I will happily write snappy, over-the-top features
about bands who deserve to be in print, not bands who
can afford free T-shirts and full-page ads.

I coast on this fantasy for a week or so, until the issue
of *Screamer* with my review in it hits the stands. I grab five

copies from the stack, eager to preserve my masterpiece—until I see that all of my goofy points, most of my biting one-liners, and roughly half of my words have been edited out. The review as published basically says that I can tell from their fabulous ballad "Emotion Number One (Cry)" that Wikked Gypsy is destined to be huge, simply *hyooge*, but that they need just a *leetle* work before their inevitable rise to superstardom can commence.

I am livid. I call Terri Ann, wondering—nay, demanding—what the fuck! Terri Ann is unapologetic, reminding me that Wikked Gypsy's manager *has* purchased not one, but four full-page ads for his band and that my review was "unprofessional" and "too mean." Not only that, but even the toned-down version has already generated a slew of nasty phone calls, from both the band's management and their groupies, and I should probably stay off the Strip for a few days if I didn't want my hair pulled or a drink thrown in my face.

Humph! Well, if Wikked Gypsy is indicative of what the Sunset Strip has to offer, I don't feel particularly sorry about missing a few nights of pseudo-entertainment. Instead, I hole up in my tiny apartment with a six-pack of beer and a twelve-pack of diet-busting Little Debbie Swiss Cake Rolls, writing up a lengthy guide to the Sunset Strip from the point of view of a smart-ass nerd girl would-be rocker that makes my Wikked Gypsy review look drier than a doctoral dissertation. I have no idea what I'm going to do with it, maybe nothing, but the very act of writing it makes me feel better, an intellectual and creative *fuck you* to a scene that wouldn't know Boy Howdy if he bit them on the ass.

Q: *Whoa! So you mean to tell me that music journalism is not unbiased? You mean the bands that get good reviews aren't necessarily good?*

A: *And there is no Easter Bunny, and Mister Green Jeans was not Frank Zappa's father. It's a sad story, but a true story. Think about this, too—if it's this bad on the level of small-time local hair bands, think about the sheer amount of bank it would take to get good press in a national magazine or on MTV. And you thought it was all about talent.*

When I finally make my reentry into the world of the Strip, I do so with protection. Raelynn, my across-the-cubicle partner in crime, is the only person in my office who will brave the places where I hang out on the weekends. A trash-talking divorcée from the wrong side of the tracks in Bixby, Oklahoma, Raelynn has big red hair in a shade not provided by nature, bountiful good ol' girl curves, and a smarter mouth and a quicker left jab than I do. Raelynn also has a pack-a-day habit, and she and I spend our coffee breaks out on the fire escape so she can smoke and we both can grouse; a double write-up documenting the frequency of our grousefests gets us dubbed "Bad Attitude Editor Woman and her sidekick, Stogie Girl" by our coworkers in a cartoon posted on the office wall. I am secure with Raelynn by my side, knowing that if I am recognized as the cruel bitch who pointed out that the Emperor's clothes were really fucking cheesy, no one will get in more than one good hit before Raelynn takes them out.

"Look at this crap," I tell Raelynn, pointing around the smoky nightclub at the surrounding hairfest. "I mean, they expect me not to make fun of this somehow."

Raelynn sips her beer and nods. "Well, they do seem like they're all taking it really seriously. Check this guy out." She jerks her head back, indicating the guy standing behind her. He's chatting up two girls simultaneously, his nasal British accent whinging its way into our conversation over the din of Faster Pussycat. "What is that jacket he's wearing?" I lean in and squint at the back of his leather jacket. Instead of the requisite spikes and studs, his jacket is embellished with rows of tiny rhinestones. Incomplete rows; on close inspection, there are a couple of bald spots where rhinestones used to be but now there is nothing but smooth leather.

"I think he's shedding."

"Really? Let me help him out." Raelynn reaches back with one long acrylic nail and ever so gently—*thwick*—flicks a rhinestone off the back of his shoulder. I stifle a giggle and she flicks another one, and another, and another. He doesn't feel a thing, and within seconds he's missing a patch the size of a silver dollar. "Now, what were we talking about?"

"All of this crap. I'm supposed to act like these bands are doing something original and gripping when all they're doing is knocking off Guns N' Roses for the umpteenth time." My eyes wander to the bar's bouncer, muscle-bound and Titian-haired, all jawbone and shoulders in a snakeskin-trimmed jacket. "Don't get me wrong, I like a long-haired guy in a leather jacket as much as anybody," I add, motioning to the bouncer, "but that doesn't make him Jimmy Page, you know?"

Raelynn agrees. "I like Moon Pies, but that doesn't make 'em caviar." I understand what she's saying, I think. Either way, I am beginning to question my own reasons for coming to Los Angeles in the first place. I latched onto Guns N' Roses after four years mired in frat parties and college radio, desperate for something raunchy, dirty, and loud. When I saw that magazine cover in the Tinee Giant convenience store, I could tell that this was as far as I could get from William and Mary, and I dove at it. Maybe I should have waited for the pendulum to stop swinging before I made up my mind what to do with the rest of my life. Maybe I should have gone to New York and tried to get in with *Spin*; at least they understand irony and sarcasm there. Or maybe, and I shudder to think it, I'm just as bad as the paisley-wearing college-radio kids I hated so much, and I'm just one more egghead, too smart to rock 'n' roll. I down the rest of my beer, refusing to even let such a thought linger. I can rock 'n' roll with the best of them. I'm as greasy as the next headbanger. *Totally.*

"Hey, look out," I say, tilting my empty bottle toward a tall, balding guy walking toward us with two beers. He looks as out of place as I feel, in a tweedy jacket and khaki pants, but it doesn't seem to bug him. In fact, he looks oddly smug as he crosses the floor and hands us each a bottle of Budweiser.

"Evening, ladies, how are we?" I take the beer— I'm not proud, I'm thirsty—and look at Raelynn like *can you believe this clown?* To my surprise, she's *smiling*, and nodding her head in recognition as she toasts him with her new beer.

"Well, hey! Frasier Crane!" He smiles at me, still smug, looking all proud, and toasts her back with his beer.

"What, you know this guy?" Now I'm all confused. Raelynn just moved here from Oklahoma; how come she knows more people than I do already?

"He's Frasier Crane! You know, from *Cheers*!"

Ohhh. I've heard of *Cheers*; it's one of those shows that everybody but me has seen. It's not that I'm a media snob, far from it—in fact, if she had said "Hey, it's Sideshow Bob," I would have known exactly who she was talking about. It's just that if my television is on, it's on music videos. Somehow I just seem to miss out on all of the prime time phenomena. I never saw *The Cosby Show* until it hit syndication, and even then I only saw bits and pieces. I just don't have the attention span for a half-hour sitcom.

"That it is, that it is," Frasier Crane acknowledges, and I hide my embarrassment at not recognizing him behind a few quick gulps from the bottle.

"How's Norm?" Raelynn seems amused by the whole situation. Even though Frasier Crane can't tell, I can see that Raelynn is actually mocking him just a little. I know her tone well enough to pick up on it, but he doesn't. Speaking of picking up on things, Frasier doesn't waste any time getting to the point.

"He's fine. Tell you what, ladies, I've got a car out front, and my house is a lot more comfortable than this dive, so drink up and let's head over there and continue the party, shall we?"

"Just like that, huh?" Raelynn is still smiling, which tricks Frasier Crane into thinking she's being friendly. Not hardly. He nods and waves his arm, motioning toward the door. Raelynn looks at me and laughs, shaking her head. "Frasier Crane is a big old pig! That is too much!" She makes a disgusted face and scootches her chair around so her back is to him. This must happen with some frequency, because rather than keep trying to convince us, Frasier Crane shrugs his shoulders and heads back across the bar, two beers poorer but apparently undaunted.

"I just don't know," I tell Raelynn, back to the original topic after our prime-time interlude. "I don't know if I'm cut out to write the stuff they expect me to write out here. It's almost like creativity is a handicap."

"Hollywood is turning out to be a lot like Bixby," she agrees. I almost wish Hollywood were a little more like Richmond. At least I was allowed to be sarcastic there. In any case, I resolve to try and find a position with a magazine where I'm allowed to write maybe not 100 percent Lester Bangs style but at least with a little humor and some semblance of journalistic ethics. I decide to send my Sunset Strip piece to *Spin* and see if maybe they could at least tell me if it's worth anything. I don't have any illusions about them printing it or hiring me. I'm just running out of options in Hollywood, and New York is as far from Hollywood as Hollywood is from William and Mary.

"Well, ladies, I bid you farewell!" This from Frasier Crane, headed toward the door with two giggling girls in tow who resemble lower-rent versions of Raelynn and myself—and, with all due respect to Raelynn, wherever she may be, we are not exactly Park Place and Boardwalk to begin with.

"It's nice to see that some of the patrons of this establishment appreciate a good offer when it comes their way!" The party girls have continued toward the door but Frasier Crane is still calling across the bar at us, making sure we see him leave. If I didn't know better, I'd think old Frasier Crane's feelings were a little bit hurt. Somewhere, deep down inside of all of us, is that kid who got picked last for dodgeball every time.

"Later, Fraze," Raelynn calls cheerily, waving at him as he finally turns to go. I shake my head, wondering if I can edit this story for my parents as I am sure they know *Cheers*. In the meantime, though, poor Frasier Crane is out of sight, out of mind, as two raging hair farmers are motioning to us from the far side of the room. Without even tactfully waiting to make sure our spurned suitor has left the building, we pick up our free drinks and head over to meet our new friends.

Later that night, after the hair farmers have been deemed unworthy of further investigation and the free beer has stopped flowing, Raelynn and I sit at a Winchell's doughnut shop on Hollywood, sipping coffee and commiserating about what brought us to Hollywood in the first place. I tell my sad tale of woe, the Tinee Giant and Axl Rose and the all-poster format, and then it is Raelynn's turn.

"I grew up in a town so small that the only thing I could

111

picture myself doing was working at the Tastee-Freez," Rae-lynn says between bites of her doughnut. "I felt like I was destined for something big, and the Tastee-Freez was the biggest thing in town. So that's what I did, for ten years."

"Was that before or after you got married?" I know that Raelynn came to Los Angeles right after her divorce was final. This in and of itself makes her seem incredibly worldly and, well, old to me, even though she isn't even thirty. In my narrow little worldview, I have very few contemporaries who are divorced. In fact, I have one, and she is it.

"Oh, after. Everything I did was after I got married. My wedding was three weeks after my high school gradua-tion." She picks at her doughnut, then wraps it in a napkin. "Clint was a nice guy and all, but I shouldn't have married him. What did I know?"

I nod, because I totally understand. I had the usual school-girl fantasies about me and my high school boyfriend Andy running off and getting married, setting up house downtown and raising punk rock babies. Thank God for the little bit of impulse control I do have, because otherwise where would I be right now? Married to Andy, that's where I'd be, and I have nothing but circumstance to thank for that. I was born into a family, a city, and a socioeconomic bracket where you didn't get married straight out of high school. Raelynn wasn't so lucky. And now, by some weird twist of fate, we're on parallel paths on the other side of the country, me seeking my fame and fortune as the next Lester Bangs and Raelynn as, well, honestly, I don't even know what Raelynn's plans for the future are. But here we are, anyway, a couple of white chicks sitting around eating doughnuts. All roads really do converge.

We get up and clear our table and head out to the car. We stop long enough to sneak a peek into the Thai dance hall next door, the open door tempting us but the lack of English on any of the signs making us think twice. On the stage, a female singer stands alone in a blue circle of light. She is young, pretty, and slight, wearing a silver-sequined evening gown and an elaborate updo. The club itself is gorgeous, posh, and empty but for three businessmen in the far back booth. In a particularly surreal detail, the singer seems to be singing a Thai rendition of "Crazy" by Patsy Cline. We are mesmerized.

"I guess you never do know how things are gonna turn out, even when you think you do," Raelynn says with beery sentimentality. "I mean, Jeez, look at her." Raelynn seems lost in thought for a moment, then goes on. "She probably dreamed about coming to America her whole life . . . and now look. She's singing for drunks at the—" She looks up above the door at the club name, a curving red and yellow neon vine of Thai script. Raelynn is undaunted. "At the Akka-makka-bakka-lakka Lounge."

I nod again because, again, I totally understand. In fact, I feel like that girl, only without the sequins or the Patsy Cline. Clear across the country, half a year of butt-kissing, interviewing, and paying dues, and for what? To write nice things in a free paper about a guy with a nipple ring and no last name.

Crazy indeed, I think to myself. Maybe I should move to Bixby, Oklahoma. I hear the Tastee-Freez is down a waitress.

With Hollywood less than I hoped it would be, I find myself inexplicably homesick for Richmond. There are so many little things I miss—Bill's Barbecue, and Mrs. Fearnow's Brunswick Stew in the yellow can, and highways that don't deserve the moniker "Death Ride from Hell." I am so homesick that I jump at my mother's offer to come out to visit for a week, even though I know it will be a week of tourist tours and celebrity spotting instead of drinking at hip dives and trolling for hair gods. She arrives with a list of must-see destinations, and I dutifully chauffeur her wherever she wants to go. I take her to see Johnny Carson tape, and since we're in Burbank, she takes me to IKEA for some apartment furniture—everybody wins. We do the Pacific Coast Highway and Beverly Hills, and even, God help me, the Hard Rock Cafe. At night I turn the television up loud in hopes that she won't hear the gangbangers' gunshots echoing up and down Hollywood Boulevard. One night I don't turn it up loud enough, and I come back from brushing my teeth to find her crouched by the window.

"Sssssh," she says, her eyes wide with excitement. "I think I heard a gunshot!"

"Oh, *that*," I say, trying to sound nonchalant. "That's just a truck backfiring. The Hollywood Freeway is really close!" She seems to buy it, or want to, anyway, and doesn't mention it for the rest of the visit.

The highlight of her trip is our afternoon on Rodeo Drive, not so much for the shopping, since we can't afford to buy even a Louis Vuitton keychain there, but because coming out of Harry Winston Jewelers, we run smack into

Margaux Hemingway, surrounded by a sizeable entourage and made up like a Kabuki chorus girl. As she is hustled past by her handlers, looking imperious and yet somehow just a little dazed, my mother stops and stares, literally open-mouthed, on the street corner.

"That was Margaux Hemingway," my mom hisses in a stage whisper. "And not a bra in sight!" God bless Margaux Hemingway. I always had a soft spot for her after that.

After my mom heads back to Richmond, I am still wistful, maybe even a little more so, just wishing I didn't feel like quite so much of a nerd among all the hipster goings-on. For that very reason, when GWAR comes to town to play the Hollywood Palladium, I actually go— something I never did when they played on the corner of my street in Richmond, because really, how many times can stage blood and mayonnaise be fun?

Q: *Mayonnaise?*

A: *Yep, this is another one of those things that I get to be an old fart about. "Back in my day, GWAR didn't have all those fancy sets and special effects! They just threw mayonnaise on us from giant food service jars! And we liked it!"*

Oh, and for those of you who somehow missed the whole GWAR phenomenon, they're a theatrical shock-metal band from Richmond who wear big scary costumes and create all kinds of mayhem as part of their show, drenching the audience in (gener- ally) simulated bodily fluids and acting out all manner of vio- lence and perversity onstage. The guys in GWAR started out as art students at VCU, and when I was at Open High you could catch Death Piggy, later to become GWAR, at apartment parties and hardcore matinees on any given Saturday if you were so inclined. Since the whole gorefest got old really fast, and also since I'm not all that keen on scraping dried mayonnaise out of my eyeglass frames, I was generally not inclined. I usually only went if my brother's band was on the same bill, or if it was a party with free beer. Family and free beer. I have my priorities.

But yeah, this time I actually cough up for a ticket and fight the crowds to go see GWAR in Hollywood, just because they remind me of home. Inside the sold-out Palladium, I feel like grabbing people, shaking them, all of these people swarming up toward the stage as if this is a big fat deal. "For God's sake, it's just GWAR," I want to say. "They're not serious! You're not supposed to be buying this!" Apparently no one outside of Richmond knows that this is all a big silly joke. I feel like I have seen the Emperor without his clothes, and it's just Dave Brockie from Death Piggy. I try to grab the band after the show, too, see if they want to get a beer or a taco with the hometown girl, but the roadie at the backstage door says they've already been invited to hang out with Ozzy Osbourne, and Satan knows I can't compete with that. It all just seems so surreal, like a bad fever dream—"I dreamed I was going to eat a taco with Dave Brockie, but Ozzy Osbourne showed up and wanted to hang out with him instead." I remember Dave panhandling for quarters outside Hard Times so that he could get a piece of pizza before their show. I hope Ozzy's buying. I was going to buy. It's still a little weird to see the world be aware of GWAR, something that seemed destined to be an inside Richmond joke. I probably shouldn't be so surprised; I'd realized it was getting out of hand a couple of years ago, when I was leafing through a metal magazine while my dad watched *Monday Night Football.*

"Look," I'd said, showing him the magazine. "It says here you can enter this sweepstakes and win a phone call from GWAR."

"They call here all the time," he said, unimpressed, "and I didn't even enter." He's right, too—on any given day, someone from GWAR or any number of other lesser-known Richmond bands called to hound my brother for recording advice, drum expertise, or just general musical knowledge. It's not for nothing that Stacey dubbed my brother "Richmond's Phil Spector."

My dad's reaction is equally deadpan when I tell him I paid fifteen dollars to see GWAR at the Palladium.

"The next time you come home," he threatens, "I'm going to charge you five dollars to see your brother." Funny guy, my dad. But he has a point. And I'm out fifteen dollars, dinnerless, and covered with stage blood.

✝

After the Wikked Gypsy debacle, I find myself getting fewer assignments at the weeklies. Los Angeles may be the big city, but when it comes to the metal scene, it's a small town, and everybody at all the weeklies has seen—and disapproved of—my snarky review and the resulting hate mail. On the one hand, that's not necessarily a bad thing, since one, I'm not getting paid anyway and two, since I'm now on double-secret probation I can't say anything the least bit negative, and unfortunately the bands they've been backing don't exactly inspire positive words. When I finally do get an assignment, a puff piece on a power-ballad band called—I kid you not—Spread Eagle, the finished product is so phony I almost can't bring myself to sign my name to it. A byline's a byline, though, and at this point beggars can't be choosers. I cringe and sign my name. I feel dirty when I see it in print.

Q: *So, would you say that this was where you hit rock bottom with your journalistic integrity?*

A: *Yeah—but that doesn't mean I stopped digging.*

If I'm limited to doing free publicity, I figure I might as well do it honestly. The less work I get from the magazines, the more time I spend at Around the World, where at least I feel like I'm not *pretending* to be objective. Morgan and Heather are thrilled with my newfound enthusiasm for gratis envelope stuffing and actually do start sliding some creative work my way—that is, if you consider one-paragraph press releases creative. I try, anyway.

"It is *so fantastic* to have you on board," enthuses Morgan when I turn in a typo-free press release that I could have written in my sleep. It's for Frankie Avalon's son Tony's band, and I make a big deal about rock 'n' roll pedigree and use terms like "hard rocking" and "in your face" as if I really mean them. "I can just *tell* that you're going to be an *awesome* publicist!" Morgan always sounds breathless. I think it's the spandex. I am glad to finally be writing something, but so far I've seen little evidence of the rapid advancement I was promised. Not only that, but Morgan made a big show of presenting all of the interns with personalized business cards with the company's logo on them last week, and Renee's say "Associate Publicist" underneath her name and mine don't say *anything*. I console myself with the fact that they don't say "Assistant Intern," but I am more than a little burned up.

The "Associate Publicist" cards are just one more tick mark on my growing list of gripes about Renee. I don't mind that she gets to pick swag before me; after all, she does have a year of seniority on me and the swag is really the only pay we get. I don't complain when she corrects me on proper envelope-stuffing form—glossies go in face down, then press release, then CD—because I am new to this whole envelope-stuffing thing and I yield to her superior stuffage skills (in hindsight, telling her that in a mock adulatory tone probably didn't help our relationship any, but she *was* kind of snotty about it, so . . .). Still, I try to get along with Renee. It's not easy given my propensity for the smart-ass response. But I bite my tongue and I try.

My ability to be nice to Renee eventually hits a wall. The Stud Wall, to be exact. Those of you who watch a lot of HGTV probably think I'm talking about an office-remodeling project gone wrong. I'm not. The Stud Wall is actually a legendary feature of the bathroom at Around the World. It started with an autographed picture of some forgotten but comely client, sans shirt. Other clients started adding their shirtless glossies to the wall, too, like dogs peeing on a fence. Then random musicians started appearing, culled from the stacks of magazines from which we clipped mentions and reviews of the bands on our roster. Sebastian Bach, Jon Bon Jovi, Stevie Rachelle, Blas Elias. The rule has always been that Stud Wall subjects have to be shirtless, pouting, and hot. That's the public rule, anyway. Apparently there is also an unspoken rule that I (as usual) manage to break with my first contribution to the Stud Wall.

My subject, snipped from the pages of *Rolling Stone*, is undeniably shirtless. His pecs are massive and glistening and his biceps firm; no one could argue that he is not hot. His stage antics drive the girls wild, especially when they roll the giant bed out onto the stage and he does the air-humping bit. In my book, and in millions of other people's, he is unquestionably a stud. In fact, his very name is a testament his studliness; the "LL" stands for "Ladies Love." Ladies Love Cool James. LL Cool J. My first proud contribution to the Stud Wall. I tape him up in between Bret Michaels and Kip Winger and think nothing else of it. That is, until I go to powder my nose a day later and find that LL has come up missing.

After a thorough and exhaustive thirty-second search of the closet-sized bathroom, I find LL residing in the wastebasket, all by his lonesome. A fresh piece of tape and the situation is resolved. I call it a fluke and return to my envelopes. The next day, LL is gone again. This time the wastebasket is empty. I begin to get suspicious, but I'm not sure who's to blame. In any case, it's a matter of principle now, and I spend the next hour digging through the mostly metal magazines in the sludge pile, finally unearthing another picture of LL in an ancient *Billboard*. I tape him back up, this time near the ceiling, with extra tape. And I wait.

LL maintains his lofty perch for over a week. I come in on Saturday to catch up on some filing and he's still there, pouting down at me, Kangol pulled over his eyes, looking studly as ever. He's there when Renee stops by to grab some CDs to take down to the DJ at Riki Rachtman's Cathouse. He's there when she goes into the bathroom to spruce up her face and prop up her cleavage for said DJ. And when she comes out, he's gone.

Just like that. Without a trace. *Probably buried in the depths of her skanky cleavage,* I think as I scowl at the LL-less Stud Wall. Poor LL! What a way to go. If he has to go buried in tits, would that they were at least nice ones, and not bigoted, over-tanned padded ones in a cheap Frederick's of Hollywood push-up bra. LL at least deserves decent foundation garments. I can't say that I am really surprised; we are, after all, talking about an eighteen-year-old Orange County strumpet who drives a Fiero with the license plate "6E Lady." Poison is probably about the deepest thing she can comprehend musically. Obviously LL is too sophisticated for her tastes, poor baby.

I don't put LL back on the wall after that. I keep my feelings about the Stud Wall incident to myself, not letting on that I know who banished LL or even that I've noticed he is gone. I let bygones be bygones for about a month. Then, one Saturday when I have the office all to myself, I slip down to the AM/PM store and buy a copy of every rap magazine they carry. On Monday, when Renee comes in to open the office, she is greeted by the new residents of the Around the World Stud Wall Mach 2 in all their Nubian glory. To those who would argue that the Flava Flav foldout poster was a poor choice for a centerpiece, well, I say you just don't get his charm, *boyeeeeee*.

Soon after the Stud Wall Segregation incident, the bathroom is painted a lovely teal and two framed prints of flowers are hung on what once was the Stud Wall. A note posted on the office bulletin board asks us to please not tape anything to the walls as we might peel the paint.

Lester Maddox would have been proud.

5

Idle Worship
Getting Punk'd Ten Years Before Ashton Kutcher

ey, give me another Valium." I nudge Raelynn's elbow, causing the eyeliner she's applying to streak up her temple, making her look like a pissed-off Cleopatra in leather.

"Why? We just had one." We've been at Boardner's since eight o'clock, drinking beer and popping the Valium that Raelynn's well-meaning doctor prescribed to carry her through her divorce. I grew up hearing my elderly aunts advising one another to "take a Valium and go lie down" whenever things got stressful—and in a house full of elderly Lebanese women, that's often—but I never knew firsthand what a magical equation that was until I met Raelynn and availed myself of her generosity and open-ended prescription. A Valium makes me feel stress-free and laid back no matter what's going on around me. A Valium and a beer makes me feel stress-free and charming. A Valium, a beer, and a shot of Jack Daniels makes me feel like Cherie Currie. I'm wondering how I made it this far without trying it.

Q: *So has Raelynn corrupted you into mixing Valium with your beer?*

123

A: *Given my family mantra, Valium and I have been on a collision course since day one. If it hadn't been Raelynn, it would have been a little old Lebanese woman in a housecoat. Besides, I'm a big girl, and the bad decisions I make are wholly my own.*

"Well, I'm feeling like the crowd is particularly stupid tonight." The collective IQ at Boardner's isn't usually Mensa level, but tonight it feels like we're dealing with, well, some very special people. So far the only guy who's even asked for my number was wearing pancake foundation over his acne and a silver lamé shirt over his paunch. No-thank-you city. We're hiding in the bathroom now, nursing our beers and hiding from Pancake and his friend, who haven't gotten the not-so-veiled brush-offs we've been giving them all night. "I just want to level the playing field a little more, that's all." Raelynn gives in and hands me a blue pill, which I swallow gratefully.

"Let's go get one more beer and then leave," she suggests, and I agree. No sense hanging around if it's going to be like this all night. We make our way to the bar for two more longnecks and observe the crowd with a mixture of disappointment and amusement. Pancake and his friend have left, but no one compelling has come in since we went to hide in the bathroom and the pickings are slim. There's the red-headed bouncer, as usual, but I've given up trying to get him to talk to me. I never see him talk to anybody, so I don't feel too insulted, but it's frustrating nonetheless. I recognize a few faces from local bands, some from the pictures on the wall at Around the World and some from my brief career at the weeklies. The singer from Junkyard is nursing a whiskey at the bar; even though they had a couple of MTV hits, he's nothing exciting since he's here most every night. Definitely not one of the better nights for hair-god shopping.

"Hey, look—it's Mike Gasper!" Raelynn points across the bar to a blond guy with an eyebrow ring and tight leather pants that lace up the side. "Remember him? He sang with that band that you took me to see in North Hollywood. What were they?"

"The Red Kennedys." New in town from Boston, the Red Kennedys play heavy metal covers of Dead Kennedys songs, rewritten to make fun of Jello Biafra's left-wing politics, and are fun once. Kind of like GWAR or Dread Zeppelin. The gimmick gets old before the second side.

"I heard he went to Harvard." If this is true, he was probably more miserable than I was at William and Mary. I feel a sudden kinship with Mike Gasper and I want to go over and tell him that it's all OK now and no one will ever call him a weirdo again, but I know it's just the Valium talking so I stay put. Besides, the bevy of silicone beauties surrounding him would have been difficult, not to mention ego-crushing, to wade through.

"OK, let's go." I drain the last sip of my beer and slide off my bar stool. All dressed up and no one to do. We had really gone for broke tonight, too. Raelynn looked lovely in a black spandex dress, leather jacket, and bolero hat, and I had trotted out my stiletto spikes for a rare weeknight appearance as the finishing touch on a fishnets-and-lace ensemble that I was sure would snare me a drummer at the very least. Nothing. We tip the bartender, say good-bye to our bouncer, who responds with a silent nod, as usual, and walk out the door.

Correction. Raelynn walks out the door. I get one foot out the door and catch my second stiletto on the threshold, sending me ass over teacups onto the sidewalk in front of my bouncer, the entire club, and the line of people out front.

Oh well. I've always wondered what it would feel like to get a standing ovation, and now I know. It stings, especially around the hands and knees.

✠

Raelynn wants to go to Denny's, but I want to go home and nurse my bruised ego and skinned palms, and besides, my stockings are ripped, so I take a raincheck. It hasn't been a good night and I just don't feel like making it longer. Truthfully, it hasn't been a good week, or a good month, and it's turning into a not very good year. Nine months in L.A. and all I have to show for it is torn stockings and skinned knees. Limping up to my second-floor apartment, I'm baffled to see the answering machine blinking, since nobody usually calls me at night but Raelynn, and we've been together all evening. The Valium continues to work its magic and prevents me from going into a patented Soffee oh-my-God-somebody-died frenzy (the usual catalyst for the "take a Valium and go lie down" order), and as soon as I navigate the buttons and dials on my archaic answering machine I'm treated to an unfamiliar voice identifying itself as an editor for *Spin* magazine . . . and not just any editor for *Spin* magazine but the one who was a contemporary of Lester Bangs himself, and the Ramones, and Patti Smith,

and all of my other heroes. The one whose name is synony-
mous with punk itself to anyone who knows anything about
the origins of punk rock. On my phone. Saying my name.
Me. Little old nerdy not very punk rock me.

"Hellooooooo, Anne, this is _____ _____ calling from
Spin. I read your article, your story, whatever, and, ah, I
like it. It's good. So I was calling to talk to you about it,
and you can call me back at 212-555-6789. So, yeah, that's
it. Bye."

Q: *So for all of this pedestal-putting and buildup, you're not
going to tell us his name?*

A: *If you're someone who'd be impressed by the name, you've
probably figured out who it is already. If you're not, it's really
not worth me risking a lawsuit over it now, is it?*

Holy fucking shit. A crude response, yes, but the only
one my brain can manage right now. Even the Valium can't
keep me calm through this. That is one of my only living
journalistic idols, on *my* answering machine, telling me *my
story* is good. Take that, *Screamer!* Put that in your pipe and
smoke it, *Hollywood Rocks!* Stuff *that* in your envelope,
Around the World! I hop around the apartment gleefully, in
between pushing the "play" button over and over again,
pausing just long enough to scrawl his number on the back
of a nearby copy of *Rock City News.* I probably have another
fifteen minutes before Raelynn gets home so I can call her
and tell her, and even then I am going to have to explain
who he is and why this is such a big damn deal. With the

time difference, it's two A.M. in Virginia, and a weeknight to boot, so I kindly refrain from calling my parents or my friends at home—well, except for Stacey, and the only reason I make an exception in her case is because I know she'll be almost as excited as I am.

"Dude! I know it's late."

"It's fucking two in the morning!"

"Yeah, but this can't wait."

"You'd better be calling to tell me you're pregnant with Rikki Rocket's secret love child." Ever since she mistook them for women, Stacey has had a totally ironic fascination with Poison. She doesn't listen to their music but she has a patch sewn on her Let's Active jacket and a "Talk Dirty to Me" sticker on her car. She asks me weekly if I've met them yet.

"No, *dude* . . . guess who I have a message from on my answering machine?" I can't wait for her to guess, and besides, I already know she will guess C. C. DeVille. I tell her.

"You've gotta be fucking kidding me!" Now she's wide awake and has forgotten all about Poison. I tell her the whole story and sit back and bask in her jealousy and awe.

Q: *Why are you making such a big deal about this guy?*

A: *For those who were not raised worshipping at the altar of punk rock journalism, imagine I were a horror writer who'd gotten a call from Stephen King. No, Edgar Allan Poe. Kinda like that.*

"So did you call him back?"

"Dude, it's like, two."

"No shit. We've discussed that. And stop calling me dude there, *bro*." Stacey doesn't hesitate to pick on me about my conversion from punk rock to mainstream metal. I don't take offense; it's not for nothing that we have watched *This Is Spinal Tap* together on three separate occasions. Both of our irony meters go to eleven.

"I think I'm gonna call him tomorrow afternoon." I make a mental note to get some more Valium from Rae-lynn. "You think he'll print my story?"

"That would be *totally rad*."

"Dude. Rad is, like, last year. What it would be is *way cool*."

"Yeah, it would. And cut me some slack—this is Richmond. It takes a while for the slang to trickle back here." She's not kidding. Everything cool here will be cool in Richmond next year or the year after, which is why hair metal was practically over by the time I got here—I hadn't accounted for lag time.

"I'll call you after and tell you what he says."

"Can't you just put me on the three-way? I promise I'll be quiet."

"Yeah, right." Stacey doesn't do quiet very well. I found that out my junior year, when she announced during her overnight show on WCWM that I'd just called in a request for the Velvet Underground from the off-campus apartment of the president of the College Democrats. After two years of turning away all comers, I'd finally given in and slept with one due to his sheer persistence. Stacey made enough not-so-sly references to the nature of my visit that his *real* girlfriend, who happened to be listening, stormed over in her pajamas and turned a merely mediocre evening into a humiliating one.

"OK. But don't forget to call me. And say hi to Nikki Sixx!" Stacey knows I don't run with the big dogs, but Los Angeles is still so glam compared to Richmond that I might as well. Even the singer for Junkyard impresses Richmond. Not me. I've been in Hollywood almost a year now, and I'm harder to impress than I used to be.

Harder, but not impossible. I listen to the message five more times before I finally go to bed.

✠

When I finally screw up my courage to call back The Idol the next afternoon, I get his answering machine. Deep down, I'm relieved, and I start to leave my name and number when I hear a click and then a paroxysm of coughing.

"Hold on." More coughing. I wait, for about a minute. Finally, the coughing subsides into a low, phlegmy growl.

"Hhhhhhhhello, *Anne*." He says my name like it's something dirty. Awfully punk rock. Good thing he can't see me grinning like a teenybopper at the phone.

"So this *thing* you wrote. I like it."

"Thanks," I say dumbly. Fortunately, my end of the conversation is not that important to him, and he keeps talking.

"It won't really work for *Spin*, you know, too regional for our demographic . . ." I want to take a moment here to ponder the fact that one of the *original* punks just used the word *demographic* without irony, but he keeps talking. "But I think you have something good here, and I definitely would like to see more of what you've got."

"I have some clips, I could mail them today." I am fairly levitating with delight.

"No, fuck that. I'm actually going to *be* in Los Angeles for a few weeks, and I was thinking that if you wanted to work out a *deal* where I could critique some writing for you in exchange for some typing and, you know, things of that *nature,* we might be able to come to an agreement that would be *mutually beneficial.*" Again, he manages to make it sound filthy. I agree immediately to be his assistant when he comes to L.A. He'll be arriving a week from Saturday and will call me when he gets into town.

"And Anne?"

"Yes?"

"What are you wearing right now?"

✠

Between Andrew at work and Stacey calling constantly from Richmond, I am whipped into a frenzy by the eve of The Idol's arrival date. I'm thrilled that I have two friends who are as excited as I am, if not more, but it's not doing my nerves any good. Next to Lester Bangs rising from the dead and asking me to be his intern, this is about as serious an *in* as I could get. I've only been reading The Idol's stuff since *middle school,* and now he's an editor at the biggest magazine besides *Rolling Stone* and he's calling me and asking me to be his assistant. Thank God for Raelynn, her

Valium, and the fact that she has no idea who he is and couldn't care less. She looks at the one picture of him I found on the editors page of *Spin*, deems him "skeevy," and proceeds to make the skeevy face every time I mention his name.

"So what time is the Skeevster pulling into town?" she asks over cocktails—OK, tallboys—at my apartment Friday night. We're dressing and making up for Boardner's, where everybody knows our name and they're always glad we came, except for the redheaded bouncer, the other girls, and some of the snootier hair gods. Some people are glad we came, anyway.

"I dunno. He's gonna call me. I need to get home early so I don't look all *ruined*," I say in my best Ed Grimley voice. It's hard to pull off Ed Grimley in a black stretch velvet halter and leopard-skin skirt, but I do my best.

"Aw, man, does that mean no after parties?" Raelynn is getting very addicted to the after parties, the random, spontaneously occurring house parties that happen when the bars close down. It's getting so that Boardner's is more the appetizer than the main event. At the after parties, the crowd is smaller, drunker, and less choosy than the crowd at the bar, and the beer is free for as long as it lasts. I dig the after parties; they remind me of my high school days in Richmond, when Andy and all of his friends worked at restaurants and we would all meet up at floating speakeasies after everyone got off work at two. This is all new and exotic to Raelynn. There weren't even any bars to close down in Bixby, much less after parties. But I am adamant.

"No after parties. I want to be in at one at the latest. Seriously."

Raelynn pouts and pokes at her hair with a rat-tail comb. "You know, tonight is probably going to be the one night Red comes to the after party, too."

"No, it's not. He never comes to any of them." Our favorite bouncer has become something of a legend. He is the Holy Grail of hair gods, gorgeous, perfect, and unattainable. We can't even get his name.

"Well, Mike Gasper at least," Raelynn concedes. She is hardly selling the idea.

"Raelynn, Mike Gasper is at every party, every night," I remind her. After all, now that everyone has seen the Red Kennedys at least once, the market is saturated and he's got a lot more time for drinking beer and picking up girls. I figure he has two months to get a new gimmick before the girls stop biting—but then that would leave more time for just beer. Not a thoroughly unpleasant situation, in my humble opinion.

"Those guys from MIT?"

"Which ones? Practically every guy in town is from MIT."

"Point taken." Raelynn resigns herself to the fact that, for once, we are not going to the after party. "Fine, but that means tomorrow night we start drinking early."

"Fair enough."

Q: *Now I'm confused. You guys are partying with MIT nerds? As in Massachusetts Institute of Technology? How did they get to Los Angeles, and how much fun, really, are those guys?*

A: *Although I must immediately point out that MIT nerds sound like all kinds of fun at parties—the stories I've heard, oy vey—our MIT boys come from the Musicians Institute in Hollywood. Originally known as the Guitar Institute of Technology (GIT) but now more expansive, MI, as it's supposed to be known but isn't, is a veritable Mecca for would-be hair gods and, by association, Raelynn and me. No slide rules but a lot of flying Vs and screeching solos. Heaven.*

☩

Despite my best efforts and Raelynn's full cooperation, we don't get home until almost three. Blame MIT, boys with gorgeous dark curls, and Denny's Grand Slam. In any case, when the phone rings at ten A.M. I am woefully unprepared.

"Aaaaaaanne," growls The Idol when he hears the sleep in my voice. "Chop chop. Time is money. I need a *go-getter* in this position. Are you going to let me down?"

"No, of course not," I grumble, thinking that a punk rock icon of all people should understand the urge to stay out late drinking, carousing, and availing oneself of other people's pharmaceuticals. "Just give me a minute to get ready and I'll be right over."

"Good. Make it fast. And go get me some cigarettes, Marlboro Reds, in the box, on your way. And orange juice. Fresh squeezed. None of that concentrate shit. And Anne?"

"Huh?"

"What are you wearing?"

Q: *So are you guys flirting, or is your idol just a creepy old letch?*

A: *Um, both. Neither should come as a surprise.*

☩

I arrive at The Idol's hotel loaded for bear with Marlboro Reds and fresh-squeezed orange juice. He's staying at the Highland Gardens, not exactly luxury but appropriate enough, seeing as it is the site of Janis Joplin's 1970 death by overdose. Sort of the California Chelsea if you will, at least now that the Tropicana is gone. I report to poolside per orders. It is not hard to spot my new boss. He is wearing skinny black jeans, blue brothel creepers, and a gaudy Hawaiian shirt covered with busty hula girls. His eyes are hidden behind black wraparound shades and his greased-down hair is thin and graying, as is the hair on his chest. The fact that I can tell this about his chest hair speaks volumes. He doesn't get up.

"Helloooo, *Anne*. Did you bring my cigarettes? Ah, good. Make sure you're saving the receipts on all this stuff. Lemme look at you. Yeah, that's it, turn around. Again. Hold it. You know who you look like?"

"PJ Soles?" I'm hopeful, but realistic. He shakes his head.

"Bailey Quarters. You know, from WKRP. I always liked Bailey better than Jennifer, the *whore*."

I sigh. "I've always wanted to look like Patti Smith." I know from our phone conversations that he has trysted with Patti Smith, which adds all the more to my idolatry of him.

He waves his hand. "Yeah, and all the girls who look like Patti Smith wish they looked like you." I'm not sure that's true, but it's a nice thought, anyway. He lights a cigarette and reaches for the orange juice. "So we have a lot to do. We can't waste any time. I'm working on a screenplay and I'm going to need you to type it for me. Also, there's an article for *SPIN* that's sort of on the same page—I'm *multitasking*—and I'll need you to type that up too. I'm going to give you tapes. Can you work with that?" I nod. I'm glad he talks a lot because it's still too early, and I am still too hung over, for coherent sentences. "Also, I'll need you to do some driving for me while I'm here. Not all of it; I'll be meeting up with people a lot and they'll drive. But for errands, food, smokes, all that, I need your wheels." I nod again. "And another thing. Do you know any black girls?"

"I'm sorry, what?"

"Black girls. Maybe from South Central. Or Latina girls, they'd be good too. I need to interview them for the screenplay." He goes on, describing a screenplay that sounds like *Dirty Dancing* to a hip-hop beat, about a poor but earnest girl who wants nothing more than to be a featured dancer on a *Soul Train*-esque show and finds that the path to featured dancerdom ain't no crystal stair. I listen numbly. Where are the junkies, the combat boots? Where is CBGBs and Joey Ramone? I'd even accept big hair and leather—hell, I already have. But booty shorts and disco heels? Is this guy an impostor?

I don't have too much time to wallow in my disappointment, because The Idol has a lunch date and I need to drive him there. He runs up to his room and apparently takes a bath in cheap cologne, then we're off to Johnny Rockett's on Melrose, where he introduces me to his lunch date, an ex-wife of one of his punk rock contemporaries who I remember seeing in the pages of *CREEM* more than once in an advanced state of dishabille. All of my doubts disappear, followed quickly by my hopes of actually getting to hang out with her as The Idol tells me to meet him back at his room at seven to start working on his tapes. I leave the two of them to their twelve-dollar cheeseburgers and head home, where I lunch on ramen noodles and humble pie, set to a soundtrack of the lunch date's ex.

✝

"He dictates his typing from the bathtub?" Stacey is horrified and delighted.

"I don't know if he always does. He told me to come over at seven and when I got there the door was open and he yelled for me to bring the tape recorder to him. And he was in the bathtub."

"Just naked?"

"Well, yeah." Those skinny rocker guys look an awful lot better with clothes on; toothpick legs in black jeans and boots look cavalier and dangerous. Toothpick legs in murky bathwater look terminal.

"So then what?"

"So then he dictated a bunch of stuff about some girl who works in an office and wants to be a dancer on some show called *Fresh Moves* while I sat on the toilet and held the tape recorder."

"And then?"

"And then he got out of the tub and smoked a bunch of cigarettes while he talked on the phone and I typed, and then he looked at the articles I brought over and said I was wasting my talent and I ought to write screenplays because that's where the money is, and then we fucked."

"Oh my God. You are my hero, you know that?"

"It actually sounds a lot more exciting than it was." I am more than a little bit ashamed of myself. Raelynn and I had talked while he was at lunch with the former Mrs. Punk Rock about what to do in the inevitable event that he made a pass at me. We both decided that I would sleep with him, in spite of his incontrovertible skeevitude, just so that I could say that I had. Raelynn's logic was that he was obviously using me, so it was not unethical of me to use him back. My logic was nonexistent. All I knew was that here was one of my punk rock idols and I had the opportunity to not just meet him, but, well, you know. You overlook a lot of skeeviness when you revert to starstruck teenybopper. The actual event itself was nothing if not completely overlookable, notable only for The Idol's steady commentary in the lewdest possible terms, all delivered in the skeevy what-are-you-wearing voice. He did write for *Screw* and *Oui*, a bit of trivia I remember in the middle of the act after one particularly clichéd pronouncement. Fortunately, most of the positions he prefers don't allow him to see my constantly rolling eyes. I leave these gory details out when I tell Stacey the story.

"Yeah, but now you've slept with Patti Smith by proxy." I hadn't thought of that. Of itself, it makes any amount of skeeviness worth enduring.

"That's right," I say, my back a little straighter and my self-esteem a little higher at the thought. "Anyway, I have to go back over in an hour, because the people from the studio are coming over to see how the screenplay is coming and I need to finish typing the new scene."

"I am going to touch you when you come home for Christmas," Stacey sighs contentedly. "You are so cool."

I know she is being halfway ironic, but it still confirms that I am halfway cool, and that's all I ever really wanted, anyway.

Q: *So would we be correct in assuming this would be your highest-profile tryst?*

A: *Actually, while not on par with The Idol as far as my starry-eyed girlhood days went, I did manage a brief, disastrous affair in my thirties with one of the fixtures in all of the local bands when I was a teenybopper—one of the few who had parlayed local Richmond success into big-time notoriety in a theatrical schock rock band and a major label deal. (Much as with The Idol, if it would impress you, you've probably figured it out already, and if it wouldn't, it's not worth the lawsuit.) Anyway, we went on a couple of dates, all very proper, nice guy, cleaned up well, and then he took me to his place. His dad's place. Where he was still living in his childhood bedroom, complete with cowboy curtains and a pirate flag on the wall.*

Because I still don't know when to give up, we went on a few more dates before he inexplicably vanished for three days, then turned up at four in the morning on a workday, admitting to a nagging crack problem that manifested itself in regular binges during which he sold everything that wasn't nailed down and hosted all-night smoking parties for dealers and prostitutes as his hapless father begged him to stop.

"I can still be your boyfriend," he reassured me. "Just don't leave your purse out around me and stuff." Just another example of cool not turning out as cool as you think it will.

For the next two weeks, my nights are spent ferrying The Idol to script meetings, dinner dates, and interviews with would-be featured dancers, and my days are spent surreptitiously typing The Idol's screenplay in between workers' compensation reports. Andrew is onto what I'm doing, but in exchange for thirdhand Sex Pistols stories and semi-juicy gossip, he's willing to pretend he doesn't see me. I honestly hope he doesn't, because the more of the screenplay I see, the more embarrassed I am for The Idol and myself. It's a patchwork of hackneyed slang and slightly outdated pop culture references, strung together with the barest thread of a plot. The paper-thin characters address each other in catchphrases: "Yo, baby! You are so def and fly!" It sounds like it was written by somebody's dad, trying too hard to sound "with it." I am literally wincing as I type. I take liberties, editing out and updating as I go, hoping he won't notice. Try as I might, there is no silk purse to be made from this tripe. After a while, I just type.

In addition, I'm beginning to bristle at the "mutually beneficial" arrangement The Idol and I have. It benefits him in that I am available twenty-four hours a day for on-call typing, cigarette-and-burger-fetching, tea brewing, chauffeuring, and, how do you say, companionship. It benefits me in that I have the privilege of telling people that it exists and little else. I've received no further writing advice or publishing help since the first night, and when I ask when we might be able to discuss it, he snaps that I'm "asking too many tedious questions" and banishes me for the night. Raelynn urges me not to go back the next day, as it seems I have little to gain by continuing our association.

"He's not helping you with your writing and he's not paying you for your work," she says bluntly. "All you're getting out of this is bad sex and carpal tunnel. Ditch him now." It's tempting. He is getting moodier by the day, snapping at me if I am not fast enough bringing him his tea or his cigarettes and sometimes refusing to speak for hours on end, just smoking and scowling on the balcony of his room. If I suggest that I leave and come back later, he flies into a snarling rage, accusing me of not being serious about this very important position and threatening to replace me with one of the Latino girls he's been interviewing for the screenplay. More than once I've considered just not answering the phone anymore when he calls.

Even Stacey agrees. "You slept with him already," she points out by way of explanation. "Now whenever anybody mentions him, I can say, 'you know, my friend Anne slept with him!' It's the same whether you did it once or a hundred times. Why do it any more than you have to?"

If I were looking at him merely as a conquest, that much would be true. I already have the Figgy Fizz bottle cap in my collection now, so I don't need to drink any more soda. But—and I think we all saw this one coming— knowing when to quit is not my forte. So even when he

flies another writer in from New York to help him on the
screenplay and she turns out to be pretty, French, and
brooding, I keep on typing, fetching, and driving. I actually
like the new writer, Therese, and am glad to have someone
around to keep me company when he goes into one of his
sulking fits (which happen more and more often as his
deadline draws closer). One night, when he is so deep into
a fit that he won't speak to either one of us, I decide that
Therese could benefit from the same therapy that has been
aiding Raelynn and me for months. We leave The Idol pouting in the bathtub and head to Boardner's, armed with Valium and the hopes of using Therese's exotic charm to cadge
many free drinks from hair gods.

"So how long have you known the Skeevster?" Raelynn
dislikes The Idol so much that she refuses to even use his
name in conversation. I think Therese chalks it up to the
language barrier and takes it in stride.

"I've worked with him on many projects, for about five
years," she says, squeezing a lime into her beer, "but we
actually met through his wife—she is an old friend of mine."

"His *wife*?" I figure this is a language thing too, and
maybe she means ex-wife. Raelynn is not going to leave it
up to chance.

"Is he married now?"

"Oh, yes," Therese says innocently. "His wife is very
sweet. She drove me to the airport to come here. I hope
you can meet her someday."

"Me too," says Raelynn with a shit-eating grin, and I
kick her under the table. This is not funny to me. There is a
code, a girl code, which not all girls respect but that I do

without reserve. That code is that married men are off-limits. I might not be Sandra Dee, but even I draw the line somewhere, and for me that somewhere is at other women's husbands. Or so I thought.

I excuse myself and leave Raelynn and Therese chatting up two Canadian rocker-tourists. Screeching around corners and flying through yellow lights, I am at the Highland Gardens within minutes . . . and I am pissed.

"So why didn't you tell me you were married," I glower at the still-soaking Skeevster. He does not seem to be the least bit surprised that Therese ratted him out, nor is he the least bit apologetic or ashamed.

"Come on, *Aaaaaaaanne*," he whines. "What did you think? That I was going to marry you? Take you away from all this?" I roll my eyes. That's not what I thought at all . . . at least, not after I got to know him. Maybe in the week leading up to his arrival I wove some fantasies, but his reality left little room for doubt.

"I didn't ask you for *anything*," I spit, "and the only thing I *expected* was that you would help me with my writing, because you *offered*. I guess I was stupid enough to assume you'd be up front with me about anything, since you're obviously not a man of your word. I don't know why I even . . ."

At this point I stop talking, because The Idol begins sinking slowly under the murky bathwater until he is completely submerged. After about half a minute, his head slowly breaks the surface, brows beetled, hair plastered down around his ears. He reaches out of the tub for the most recent pack of Marlboros I brought him, shakes one out and lights it, then looks at me scornfully and blows smoke through his nostrils in my direction.

"A man of my word? Look at who you're talking to here."

Touché. Expecting the original punk to be a man of honor is like expecting intelligence and wit to get me far in Hollywood. I turn on the heel of my silver-trimmed cowboy boots and walk out of the Highland Gardens, a little older, a little wiser, and not as much cooler as I thought I'd be.

✝

"He *what?*" Stacey is thrilled and disgusted at the latest turn of events in the Punk Rock Idol soap opera. Not the wife; we covered that a week ago. This is new stuff that's affecting me a lot more directly than a cross-country spouse.

"He skipped town! I went over to work on the screenplay and he'd checked out! Therese left me a note saying it was nice to meet me, but he didn't leave me shit." I had a feeling that the "save your receipts" line was bullshit all along, but of course I'd saved them just in case. I'm probably out a couple of hundred bucks' worth of burgers and smokes, and a hell of a lot of time, but that's nothing compared to the people who ponied up for the screenplay. It's my understanding that, in addition to a fat advance, they'd also covered The Idol's hotel and airfare. All they had to show for it now was the first half of an incredibly lousy screenplay—and apparently, a message from The Idol saying I was still typing the other half.

"The movie people are ringing my phone off the hook. They're *pissed*." I've been afraid to answer my phone all weekend, and their messages are getting downright threatening. "*You're putting us in a very unpleasant predicament*," the last one warned ominously. "Shit, I hope they don't know where I live."

"This is like a movie," Stacey says cheerfully.

"Says you," I grumble. At least it's better than the one The Idol was writing. If there is no other silver lining here, at least I know in my heart that *Fresh Moves* will never see the light of day.

6

I, Industry Weasel
*Gabba Gabba, We Accept You,
We Accept You, One of Us*

i celebrate my first anniversary in L.A. in high style—
at Boardner's, of course, with Raelynn. It's just
another night, to be honest, and I am growing a little
tired of the routine but don't see any other way. I sense
that my days at the workers' comp firm are numbered; not
that I'm not doing a good job, though I could probably
stand to be at the office a little earlier and a little more
clear-headed. Thank God for flex time. In fact, the wheels
of workers' comp reform are already in motion, and it
seems like almost weekly another few of my fellow cube
farmers are called into Andrew's office for the bad news,
followed by the desultory desk clean out and the escorted
march to the elevator.

At Around the World, I am doing more publicity and
less envelope stuffing, thanks in part to the arrival of two
new interns who are now lower than me on the totem
pole. The bad news is that for most of my publicity assignments, I'm paired with the evil Renee, who is as thrilled
about the arrangement as I am. Not only that, but we
aren't exactly getting the plum assignments, either. Anything that Heather and Morgan don't want to do, they give
to us. Like dealing with Vinnie Vincent.

Q: *You mean Vinnie Vincent from Kiss? Vinnie Vincent Invasion Vinnie Vincent? Rock on! What's to complain about there?*

A: *Yes, that Vinnie Vincent, although in the interest of full disclosure, he was only in Kiss from late 1982 to early 1984, post-makeup—which was lucky for Vinnie, because the makeup he'd come up with for the gig was a super-cheesy silver ankh on his forehead that made him look like an Egyptian mime. Also in the interest of full disclosure, this is the same Vinnie Vincent who ghostwrote all of Joanie and Chachi's songs on* Happy Days. *Rock on indeed.*

I don't know how Renee feels about being Vinnie Vincent's publicist, but for me even his brief association with Kiss is enough to make this exciting at the outset. I was the kid in the Kiss *Destroyer* T-shirt on the playground in 1976, the one who played Gene to Melissa's Ace in the fourth-grade talent show. Lip-synching and tongue-wagging to "Rock and Roll All Night," we didn't win, but we were the coolest kids on the bus that day in our greasepaint makeup and Reynolds Wrap boots. I still have my Spirit of '76 Tour poster, my *Destroyer* jigsaw puzzle, and all four solo albums on vinyl. He could have been a roadie for a weekend and I would still be just a little impressed to be working with him.

I am dying to meet Vinnie in person, but alas, he lives up to Heather's warning that he is Howard Hughes–level reclusive. He insists on conducting all of his publicity over the phone. My disappointment knows no bounds. I have been dying to see his wig.

"That's a wig?" Raelynn squints at his publicity photo, which I brought home to inspire me while I write up his new bio. "It looks just like everybody else in the band's hair."

"That's why I want to meet him," I say evilly. "I want to *tug* it." My metalhead friends and I had laughed hysterically when Slaughter was being interviewed on *Headbanger's Ball* and told their Vinnie Vincent wig story. Former members of Vinnie's band, Dana Strum and Mark Slaughter, told host Riki Rachtman about the night they taunted Vinnie mercilessly, hoping to start a fight so they would have an excuse to quit the band. "But he wouldn't fight," they complained. "He just stood very still so his wig wouldn't fall off." The visual image of a beleaguered Vinnie Vincent standing like a statue to preserve his phony 'do was too much for us. It's still the first thing I think about every time I see his picture.

"And what did you say he calls you?"

"I'm Francine and Renee is Claudette," I sigh. "He said he wanted his publicists to be named Francine and Claudette." I've had stranger requests. I have no problem accepting a pseudonym, especially not at this late stage of my soul selling. Now that I am no longer doing any journalism and have resigned myself to my position as a whore of the industry, I've embraced the nature of the beast and given myself completely over to the dark side. I'm sporting crimson acrylic nails on my fingers—painful, and near impossible to type with, but de rigueur for industry schmoozes. Raelynn and I plopped down three hundred dollars apiece for lifetime memberships to Jenny Craig, and thanks to horrible powdered food and TV dinners we're down ten pounds each and shrinking. We'd probably shrink faster if we swore off the hard stuff, but you need something to drown your conscience when you are recommending that aspiring seventeen-year-old drummers get hair extensions. In life you have to make allowances.

"You really *are* Bobbi Fleckman now," Stacey marvels when she hears about my latest exploits, referring to Fran Drescher's pushy A&R rep in *This Is Spiñal Tap*. The reality is that I am worse: blithely telling musicians to lose twenty pounds or bleach out their hair without the first thought to the quality of their playing or the originality of their songs. Indeed, why should I encourage anyone to be creative or original when it's not going to get them half as far as a good dye job and a tight ass? I may not agree with the rules, but now that I know how the game is played, I owe it to the bands I work for to give them advice that will advance their careers, not their esteem in my eyes. Unfortunately, *my* esteem in my eyes is what's taking the beating, in spite of all of my cosmetic improvements. I am contributing to the downfall of the thing that has always meant the most to me—rock 'n' roll. I'm Brutus in a bustier.

Q: *So what makes you abandon your artistic integrity in favor of acrylic nails and Jenny Craig?*

A: *Hey, I'm just doing as the Romans do. See also Stockholm Syndrome and/or Stanford Prison Experiment. In short, I've been in Los Angeles for a year and I'm starting to forget that the rest of the world does not require acrylic nails and powdered food. It seems normal to me.*

Heather and Morgan couldn't be happier. I wish that
I thought it had anything at all to do with my talent or
intelligence; in truth it has everything to do with my
growing nails and shrinking ass. In addition to giving me
the Vinnie Vincent account and sending me out on look-
sees for upcoming local bands, they send me to a weekend
workshop put on by two major-label publicists to learn
the tricks of the trade and garner inside tips such as the
following gems:

> • If your artist has to cancel a show or an inter-
> view because, say, his father is dying or his wife is
> in labor, plant a rumor that he OD'd or is in
> detox. It will sound more rock 'n' roll.
>
> • Speaking of wives, they officially do not exist.
> Wives and girlfriends are not to be present at
> meet-and-greets or interviews because it projects
> an air of unattainability that turns off the all-
> important female fans (and female journalists,
> who publicists see as nothing more than female
> fans with press credentials and the potential to
> give good or bad press depending on how much
> the artist flirts with them).
>
> • If your artist meets a young lady at a show and
> wants to stay in touch with her but he's married,
> it is your duty to relay messages back and forth
> without informing his wife. Your loyalty is to your
> band and their fans, not their wives.

And my favorite:

> • Encourage your bands to bathe before interviews.
> Good-smelling bands always get better press.

We've come a long way from the days when Jim Morrison wore the same leather pants until they could walk on their own, but whether we're traveling in the right direction remains to be seen. I find myself wistful for the days when I was back in Richmond, writing honest reviews about bands that nobody was being paid to groom. Besides, if I'm not writing, what am I doing here?

"You're going to love them," I enthuse on the phone to a journalist I'm inviting to see one of our bands. "They're young and grungy. Think New Kids meet Nirvana." *New Kids meet Nirvana?* Did I just say that? It's no wonder I've moved on from Raelynn's Valium to everyone else in the office's everything else. Xanax, Darvocet, Percocet, anything with the familiar "no cocktails" symbol on the side, I've got an open call in the office for any old prescriptions that anyone has lying around. I rationalize my new pastime with the comforting notion that somewhere, a doctor prescribed these to help someone, so they must be inherently helpful and therefore good for me. It keeps me from feeling like an after-school special waiting to happen.

As Halloween draws closer, I realize that I haven't run into Glenn Danzig in *weeks*. He's become something of a Kilroy in my Fellini-esque Hollywood life, popping his head up unexpectedly everywhere from the taco place on the corner to the bookstore five miles down the road. Preparing for Halloween is probably a major undertaking for Glenn Danzig, I figure, like Christmas for Santa Claus. It occurs to me that my newfound schmoozing skills might be just the thing I need to scare up some memorable Halloween fun. In the break room at my day job, I place a quick call to Def American records and put on my best Bobbi Fleckman voice.

"Yeah, *hiiiiiiiiiiii,* this is Anne over at Around the World. We're just putting together our October schedule and we need to know if Danzig has any special appearances planned for Halloween."

"They sure do, they're playing at Riki Rachtman's Halloween party at Club Spice."

"OK, got it! Thanks so much!" *Hmmmmmm.* A private party. Tough, but still doable. At least it's Riki Rachtman's party and not somebody utterly untouchable like, say, Axl Rose or Tommy Lee. In spite of his tattoo sleeve and his famous friends, Riki Rachtman is enough of a nebbish that I might be able to swing this, even as an assistant intern. I make a quick call to Around the World and, through one of the naive and eager-to-please new interns, am able to round up Riki Rachtman's phone number with a minimum of fuss. The next call deserves an audience, so I knock on Andrew's door to make sure he's not firing anyone and invite myself in.

"You're gonna want to see this. Give me your phone." Andrew doesn't ask questions but slides his phone across the desk and leans in. I dial the number and become Bobbi again.

"Hi! May I speak to Riki Rachtman, please? It's Anne from Around the World." Andrew stifles a snicker. Riki Rachtman is high camp, right up there with Poison. The fact that his number was dialed from Andrew's phone will be a great story for the Dresden Room tonight. I hold for a minute and then I'm on the line with Riki himself.

"Riki, hi, it's Anne from Around the World!" The first rule of schmoozing is to act like you're following up on an earlier schmooze. The schmoozee will assume his memory is faulty and will be too embarrassed not to go along with whatever you're saying. Riki plays into it like a champ.

"Hey, look, I'm just checking up on the guest list for the Halloween party. You've got me covered, right? Yeah, Anne with an E. S-O-F-F-E-E. Uh-huh. No, I totally understand, yeah, it's late and I figured your list would be pretty full. One is fine, yeah. Really. And thanks again for everything! Catch you later, Riki!"

"Wow." Andrew has never seen me schmooze before. "How much did you get for it?"

"For what?"

"Your soul." I start to get indignant but realize that I did, in fact, just kiss Riki Rachtman's butt for Danzig tickets. I don't have a leg to stand on. I settle for flicking a paper clip at him and head back to my desk. I want to celebrate my score, drink to my superior schmoozability, and bask in the thought of being on the guest list for a private party with Danzig. Unfortunately, though, there are gardeners and truck drivers out there waiting for their workers' comp. Rock 'n' roll will have to wait until after five o'clock.

✝

The night of Riki's party, I leave work early to prepare. I do my makeup flawlessly, don my best seamed fishnets and my pointiest boots, and tease out my hair even bigger than

usual. I pull on my requisite leather biker jacket and chase
down two Valiums with a bottle of Budweiser to take the
edge off my nerdiness. I'm not thrilled with the results of
my metal makeover; I never am, really—all the hairspray
and Wonder bras in the world don't change the fact that I
am shorter in the leg and fuller in the face than I need to
be to really hold my own in Hollywood. I used to think that
a high IQ, quick wit, and general rocker chick attitude
helped my case; I mean, come on, Joan Jett, Lita Ford,
right? This is where the Runaways made history! Hollywood's gotta love rocker chicks who are more smartass
than sexy, right? It was, cheesily enough, an interview with
Vince Neil that made me realize how times have changed in
Hollywood. "The perfect Hollywood girl," he opined, "can
party all night and still get up at six A.M. and go to the
gym!" In other words, *keep up with me at the bar, baby, but
don't let it go to your ass or you're outta here!* Today, the perfect Hollywood girl has less in common with Lester Bangs
than she does with Suzanne Somers, and that disheartens
me enough that I chug one more beer before leaving the
apartment, which would make me a little more perfect in
Vince Neil's eyes were it not for the fact that I have no
intention of getting up at dawn to Stairmaster it off. After a
quick call to leave a message on Stacey's phone—"I'll tell
CC you said hi"—I'm off to Club Spice to party with the
lesser gods of rock 'n' roll.

   As promised, my name is on the list and I have no
problems getting in. I take this as a sign that it's going to be
a good night. Even back in Richmond, when having my
name on the list meant little more than getting a free show

from guys my brother hung out with after school, there has always been something ego-boosting about watching the doorman scan down the list for my name, find it, and wave me in. Maybe it just makes me feel a little more like Lester Bangs for a second. Tonight the victory is extra sweet because not only is it a private party, but it is being hosted by someone my friends at home have heard of and I successfully crashed it. Not to mention the presence of Danzig, which makes me feel just almost too cool to comprehend. Glancing around inside the club, I see a few Halloween costumes but mostly a lot of black leather and jeans, typical Hollywood. Everyone is too cool to be bothered to dress up, present company not excepted. I grab a drink and look around for Riki or any of the guys from Danzig; spotting neither, I make myself at home at the bar to wait for the show. It's times like this I wish I smoked, just to give me something to do between drinks. I chat with the bartender instead, trading nerdy bar jokes for drinks and asking after Riki—after all, beneath the leather, fishnets, and Valium I am a good southern girl and a good southern girl always thanks her host.

"He's somewhere around here," the bartender says, peering through the crowd. "He's dressed as Michelangelo."

Points for Riki fucking Rachtman! I didn't know he had it in him, though I should have. Short, semitic, and chubby, he always did set the nerd-o-meter off just a little, all those nights on *Headbanger's Ball*. Surely if he were truly cool he'd be in a band instead of hosting a show *about* bands. Michelangelo! I can't wait to tell Stacey and Andrew that Gabba Gabba, Riki is one of us, as evidenced by his

appreciation for the fine arts. Only a nerd would dress up
as a famous artist for Halloween.

My nerd pride moment is interrupted by the familiar
thud of mikes being checked, so I bid the bartender
farewell and slide down the wall to the front of the room
to get a good vantage point for the show. The stage is set up
with a drum set and three wooden stools surrounded by
jack-o'-lanterns; odd, but it is Halloween so anything can
happen. From the wall, I move to the side of the stage, and
then to the stage steps, where I squeeze myself up against
the side of a Marshall amp, my black leather jacket camou-
flaging me nicely against the watchful eyes of the bouncers.
From my seat, I have a great view of the stage and a not-
bad view of the audience. Clearly the best seat in the
house. As I sit behind the amp congratulating myself on my
good fortune, a Teenage Mutant Ninja Turtle takes the stage
and fumbles with one of the mike stands, trying to get his
giant green turtle hands around the mike.

"Happy Halloween, everybody!" Riki Rachtman's muffled
voice comes out of the Turtle's huge green head, and suddenly
I feel incredibly nerdy. *That* Michelangelo. Oh well. I should
have known it was too good to be true. The turtle yells a few
excited but unintelligible phrases and then claps his big green
hands together and stumbles off the stage. Danzig comes out
carrying, improbably, acoustic instruments. Glenn Danzig, for
all his fishnet-shirt wearing, buff-Jersey-metal-guy posing, is
still just about the hottest thing since Atomic Fireballs in my
Halloween book. After thanking the now not quite so cool
Riki and wishing the crowd a happy Halloween, the band
launches into an acoustic version of "Killer Wolf."

When I went to that Danzig show in Arizona, I'll admit, I went as a scoffer. I was there to be ironic and snigger behind my hand. Danzig is a little over-the-top with their inverted crosses and horned skulls, n'est ce pas? They lend themselves to the ironically superior. But this? This is fucking *great*. This rocks in a completely not ironic and down-in-the-gut *fuck yeah* way. Atta boy, Glenny-boo. I knew you had it in you. After all, you were the man behind the Misfits, no matter what Jerry Only says. Electric, these songs are cool and all, but acoustic, the blues influences shine through in spades. They don't even sound like the same songs, just a lot of thumping and twanging and evil Mississippi growls—never mind that Glenn is from Lodi, New Jersey. He must have met the devil at the crossroads after all. I lean back against the amp and feel the chords vibrate through my bones. This is why I stay here. This is what makes it all worth it. Nothing like this in Virginia, that's for damn sure.

Danzig rolls through acoustic versions of a bunch of their songs, bass-thumping, twangy-stringed versions that rock harder than the electric versions ever dreamed of rocking. Just when I am about to throw irony to the wind and declare Danzig my favorite band of all time, they launch into "One Night with You" with Glenn Danzig doing a spot-on Elvis Presley that turns me into Shelley Fabares right on the spot. When Glenn curls his upper lip and howls, "Now I know that life without you/has been too lonely too long," no amount of Valium can make me cool. I melt into a quivering puddle of nerdiness. That's how cool this is. Heavy metal Elvis. It's like a great dream I'm having, only I'm really here!

While I am still recovering from the Elvis—and by recovering I mean planning the Danzig shrine I am going to build in my apartment when I get home—Glenn Danzig announces in his hoarse Jersey growl that he wants to do some of his favorite songs for us. I brace for maybe Misfits, New York Dolls, or if God is truly good, more Elvis, but even that can't hold a black candle to what I get. Blues. Real live Mississippi motherfucking blues. "Seventh Son." "Spoonful." "I'm a Man." My nerd rating is off the meter now, because I am singing along with all my heart and grinning like an idiot. Who needs the Blues Archive when you have Danzig? I should have saved myself the trip. The points that Riki Rachtman got for being a Michelangelo fan are paltry compared to the points Glenn Danzig is racking up tonight. He can wear all the silly satanic jewelry and black fishnet he wants and he's still the king of cool in my book. It's not just anybody who will get up in front of a Hollywood hair crowd at Riki Rachtman's party and do Willie Dixon songs as they ought to be done. I want to have his evil little children.

Only because this is shaping up to rival the Rolling Stones concerts on the Best Nights of My Life roster do I commit the ultimate act of mojo selflessness. While the band is tuning up and drinking up after their blues set, preparing for the encore, I reach into the left pocket of my leather jacket and take out my John the Conqueror root. Still wrapped in the dollar bill that I twisted around it the day I got it, it has seen me halfway around the world and all the way across the country, keeping more kinds of bad mojo at bay than I will ever know. With the root in my fist, I reach over and tap Glenn Danzig on the thigh.

"Hey," I say, almost as hoarse as he is from all the singing along.

"Oh, hey," he says back. We run into each other so often that he legitimately does recognize me now, if only as that nerdy girl who may or may not be stalking him.

"Here." I hand him the balled-up bill with the root inside. He looks puzzled, unwraps it, and pokes at the shriveled root. "It's a John the Conqueror root," I say quickly, because I want to believe that he already knows this, so I can't give him a chance to ask what it is.

"Oh, man." He wraps the dollar back around it and shoves it down into his left pocket—I *knew* he'd know what to do with it. "Thanks," he says sincerely and leans over and says something to Eerie. I lean back against the speaker, content that I have done my part to protect Glenn Danzig from bad mojo as an act of gratitude for what has turned out to be the greatest Halloween ever, bar none.

Q: *So where the hell did a nerd girl like you get a John the Conqueror root?*

A: *I bought it at a place called Ye Olde Mystique Shoppe in downtown Norfolk, Virginia, when I was in college. I dragged Stacey there one Saturday when I was in the throes of a blues-induced need for a mojo of my very own. The front room is all tarot cards and numbers books, Fast Money Bingo Powder, and Love Come Quick Floor Wash—the bread-and-butter hoodoo stuff. Behind the counter, though, there are rows of unlabeled jars with creepy dry things rattling around in them. Of course, after I bought my root, I wanted to browse the cheese factor stuff, maybe* *pick up some lotto candles, or Bring Him Back soap, but because I'd bought the root, the spooky little proprietor thought I was hardcore and kept sneaking up behind me and offering me bulk deals on eye of newt and black cat bones.*

"We're going to do one more song for you guys," Glenn Danzig rasps, and Eerie thumps out the "da-*duh-duh-duh-da*" bass line that leads into "Hoochie-Coochie Man." I bob my head to the beat and sing along with the lyrics, lyrics that I've sung along with a million times before in my room, in my car, in my head.

> *I got a black cat bone*
> *I got a mojo too*

The sign of a great show is that you can't decide if you want it to last forever or if you want it to hurry up and end so you can go call everybody you know and tell them how great it was. The sign of a truly great show is when you forget everybody you know exists outside of you and the band. That is how I feel at this show tonight. It's only me, Danzig, and Riki Rachtman in a Ninja Turtle outfit—and maybe not even Riki, especially when Glenn Danzig turns around on his stool and points at me.

> *I got a John the Conqueror Root*
> *I'm gonna mess with you*

So now, for the record, I'm onstage with Danzig, and Glenn Danzig is singing directly to me. I just want to make sure we have that all on record or I might not believe it myself. And that's the way it was, October 31, 1991.

Q: *So I take it this was the greatest concert you've ever been to in your life.*

A: *Actually, it's a close race. There was this one, which is obviously right up there, and then there was my first ever Rolling Stones concert in 1981, when I was fourteen. Nobody sang to me and I didn't get to sit on the stage, but I was in the front row, and I did manage a sip from Bill Wyman's cup of birthday champagne before one of the older, stronger screaming girls wrested it away from me.*

My new authority at Around the World may get me access to Vinnie Vincent, Riki Rachtman, and some of the better swag, but unfortunately it doesn't get me into the Foundations Forum, the heavy metal industry convention put on by Concrete Marketing that is happening at the end of the summer. Those passes are a couple of hundred dollars apiece and available only to those with ironclad credentials—like Heather and Morgan. It's cold comfort that Renee doesn't get to go either. This is without a doubt the one event where I might actually get access to editors with clout, with potential, with magazines that actually cost something on the newsstand, and I can't get in. At least not through Around the World. Even though I know it's a long shot since he has so far proven himself to have no conscience whatsoever, I drop a little coin and give The Idol a call in New York. I've finally accepted that I am never going to see any of the money I was promised or any kind of actual writing assistance, but as well connected as he is, it would only take one phone call for him to get me into this convention, and damn it, the least he could do is make one call.

"You know, you didn't pay me, you didn't reimburse me, and you left me holding the bag on that whole screenplay thing," I remind him. I don't mention the wife, figuring it might take him screeching past penitent and right on into defensive. "The least you could do is get me a pass to this stupid conference."

"I'll see what I can do," he whines. "I'm not promising anything."

"Good, because I already know what your promises are worth."

"Be nice, Anne."

"I've been nice," I remind him. "Now it's your turn."

"I'll try," he says unconvincingly.

I don't expect anything to come of our conversation, which makes it seem almost like Christmas when I receive a registration packet from Foundations Forum containing a laminated badge identifying me as a writer for *Spin* magazine. Like people cherish their first baby shoes or first dollar earned or first field-goal football, I now have my first laminated pass, something I've aspired to since I was a wee girl reading *CREEM* in my green vinyl beanbag chair in my bedroom back in Richmond. I shall cherish it forever and ever.

Q: *So do you still have it?*

A: *Of course. It's hanging up on my bulletin board between my laminated belly dancer pass and my laminated sex offender facility pass. I can only imagine what will be next.*

The Foundations Forum is, itself, surprisingly not rocking. I do meet authors and publishers and the occasional rock star, and I do collect stacks and stacks of business cards and useful names. Like any other business convention, though, it is crowded and overwhelming, mainly insincere glad-handing and frantic attempts at networking that ultimately lead nowhere. How cool can you be, really, in an airport hotel convention room? I try to make the most of the opportunity, sitting in on seminars, gathering names, and handing out resumes, but honestly, I just can't wait to get home at the end of each day.

Q: *So does the convention revive any of your dashed dreams of becoming a rock journalist?*

A: *Can you see Lester Bangs schmoozing at the Airport Marriott? Me neither. While it does feel good to have a laminated pass with my name on it, the Foundations Forum turns out to be one more nail in the coffin of my CREEM dream—after all, it's four days of paid advertising for marginally talented bands with major label expense accounts.*

On the final day of the convention, I come dragging home at ten o'clock, lugging an overflowing tote bag of giveaway swag. By my estimation of what I remember throwing in over the course of the day, I have about a dozen CDs, twenty-some tapes, a handful of pens, six videotapes, a couple of T-shirts, and countless stickers and decals for bands I've never heard of. As I'm jockeying the bag to get the front door open, I manage to tip it sideways and spill half of my swag onto the front porch.

"Here, lemme get that." The guy who lives below me, a tall, blond stoner dude who's perpetually carrying a skateboard and a beer, bends down and gathers up a couple of handfuls of swag.

"Hey, sweet, Metallica! Where did you get all this stuff?"

"I was at the Foundations Forum." I hold up my laminate pass, hopefully long enough for him to read the "*Spin* magazine" beneath my name.

"You need a hand getting this stuff upstairs?"

"Yeah, that would be great. Tell you what, you can *have* the Metallica if you help me carry it up."

"Deal!"

I actually don't need any help, but my downstairs neighbor is by far not the least attractive guy in the building and I've been trying to find an excuse to get to know him. That and I don't really care too much for Metallica. Upstairs he tells me that his name is Tommy and he's a key grip. I've always wondered what it is exactly that key grips do, but talking to Tommy doesn't help much. Between his Spicoli drawl and his obvious inebriation, I'm getting very little information out of him that makes sense. He does offer to go to Mister Kim's and get us a twelve-pack, which I accept, and we spend the rest of the night drinking,

looking through the bag of swag, and trading increasingly
unintelligible comments. By the time he heads downstairs
at three A.M., we have plans to get together the next
evening and I have a warm neighborly feeling in my heart
and in my panties. California blond isn't usually my style,
but there's something charming, compelling, and familiar
about Tommy that lets me overlook his very un-rock 'n'
roll short blond hair, muscular arms, and surfer tan.

✝

Unfortunately, it doesn't take long for me to figure out that
the familiar charm Tommy has that makes me feel so at
home is, in fact, the one thing that seems to mystically draw
me to men time after time—a heroin habit. When Tommy
shows up the next night, his eyes are pinned and he immediately goes into a nod sitting on my futon in the thirty seconds it takes me to get him a beer. I do believe that if I
picked up a Manhattan phone book and flipped it open to a
page and pointed, I'd manage to point to a junkie; that's
how strong my junkie magnet is. From my first high school
boyfriend in tenth grade, fresh out of juvenile hall, to The
Idol last month, it seems every guy I ever get in my grasp is
either a current junkie or a recovering one. So far I've had
about equal luck with both types. It probably doesn't help
that I grew up with Keith Richards as my Prince Charming,
but it seems like even when I pick someone without the
trappings, the monkey jumps out and grabs me around the
neck like an old friend. Look at Exhibit A here, passed out
on my futon looking for all the world like an ad for Pacific

Sun and just as strung out as you please.

Oh, well. Don't know when to cut my losses, you know the drill by now. I kick him in the flip-flop and hand him his beer. Might as well make the most of it.

☩

Tommy and I spend the next four nights hitting the dive bars around Hollywood together—the Frolic Room, the Gaslight, the Spotlight, and, of course, Boardner's. When we're not out drinking, we're in drinking, picking up twelve-packs at Mister Kim's and holing up in my apartment watching *Barfly* over and over, because Tommy idolizes Charles Bukowski. Raelynn is unimpressed.

"Can we go out tonight, or are you going to be drinking with that nasty boy downstairs?"

"His name is Tommy," I remind her, not that she is going to use his name. It's a matter of principle.

"Well, he's nasty," she says bluntly, and then adds some incentive. "I'll buy if you come out with me. You know he's not buying."

She has a point. Except for that first night, Tommy has never bought the drinks. When he told me he was a key grip, he didn't explain that he was an out-of-work key grip, on disability due to his drug addiction. When we go out, it's always either Dutch or my treat. The fact that Tommy is the only friend I have aside from Raelynn who likes to drink as much as I do makes him worth the expense. The added convenience of having him in the apartment below me nudges him into the lead. There are other sterling qualities too that I won't go into here; suffice to say he wins on points when compared to Raelynn. There are certain things that your girlfriends just don't do for you, and those are the things that Tommy does really well. Plus I am tired of the bar scene, tired of dating, tired of not nearly measuring up to the off-duty centerfolds and pole dancers who populate the metal clubs where Raelynn and I hang out. Tommy may not be my real boyfriend, but he quacks like a duck, and that's good enough for me at this point.

Unfortunately, my ditching Raelynn for Tommy limits the places that Tommy and I can go, because I don't want to run into Raelynn out at a bar on a night when she's called and I've told her I've got other plans. It's just bad manners. Tommy suggests that we stay in, but I'm bored with my own four walls, and besides, this is *Los Angeles* for Christ's sake— you'd think there would be enough dives in a city this size for two tiny girls to avoid each other for a day or two.

"Well," Tommy says. "I've got a place that's kind of like my secret spot. I *guess* I could take you there. I don't know if you'll like it, though. It's kind of . . . *different*."

"Good different or bad different?"

"Different different. You'd have to see it to understand." With a pitch like that, how can I resist? I grab my purse and we're off to Tommy's secret place.

From the outside, the Blacklite looks remarkably like the Spotlight and the Gaslight. A main drag dive, across from the famous Tropicana Mud Wrestling bar, the Blacklite is small and unassuming with the front windows painted black and a thick curtain hanging over the front door. I wonder to myself what is so "different different" about this place. It looks just the same as everywhere else we go on any other drinking night. Tommy winks and motions for me to step back, then he sweeps the curtain aside and ushers me in.

Through the curtain lurks an altogether foreign world from what was outside, what is at the usual dives, or anything I've ever seen in my life. When we step into our other haunts, we see hair gods and hussies and the occasional B-list actor. Junkies, rockers, scenesters, and stiffs. Cigarettes and cheap perfume cloud the air, along with the occasional sweet whiff of marijuana smoke or brown liquor. The soundtrack is Guns N' Roses and Mötley Crüe (though that's been giving way lately to Nirvana, Soundgarden, and the rest of their flannel-shirted ilk). But, there are no flannel shirts on the soundtrack at the Blacklite, and the only wannabe scenester here is me. Behind this curtain is Tommy's world, which smells of stale beer and urine and is populated by geriatric barflies, aging queens, and drag queen hookers. A statuesque tranny in a Patti LaBelle chiffon concoction hangs on the arm of an Archie Bunker look-alike, chucking him under the chin and giggling. By the light of the jukebox, a barely legal lady boy in short shorts and a haltertop touches up a chipped bit of polish on his inch-long pink fingernails while Patsy Cline wails that she falls to pieces. I immediately understand what Tommy meant by "different different."

Tommy comes over and hands me a beer. "They're on the house," he says, and sticks a dollar in the jukebox. I pick a schizophrenic mix—Tammy Wynette, Heart, Blood Sweat and Tears—that somehow seems perfect for this place. Tommy points around the bar, spouting a list of names I will forget after a couple more beers. "That's Brandi . . . and Carmella . . . and Candy . . . and Desiree. The bartender's Billy and over there, that's Aunt Titty. And in the wheelchair, Miss Bunny." I peer around the darkened bar, taking in the made-up faces, their jaws angular and their lips pouting and red. I feel relaxed and I haven't even taken a Valium. It's like I'm not really here. I guess it's because I just don't figure into the dynamic here in any logical way—as a straight girl, I'm effectively invisible. Nobody looks at me, talks to me, or even seems to notice that I'm here. It gives me a strange feeling of relief. I like it.

I finish my beer and get us two more. The bartender, Billy, is genial, a red-cheeked chubby caricature of a bartender, complete with a rag over his shoulder. He gives me a shot of something sweet and syrupy, on the house, before he gets my beers. It tastes like cough syrup and makes me feel warm and happy. Maybe it is cough syrup. I don't care, I'm just glad to be here. I wander around the bar, looking at the dusty photos on the walls, the ancient Christmas lights hanging from the ceiling, and, from the corner of my eye, the patrons as they interact. I pass the Archie Bunker guy, now locked in an embrace with a gray-haired man in a faded work shirt. "You may be a fat old queen, but you're my fat old queen," the man in the work shirt says in a gravelly Brooklyn brogue. I smile at him and he winks at me, a fatherly wink, not a lecherous one. I decide that this is going to be my new hangout.

Tommy is playing darts with a couple of the senior

citizens, and I have to pee anyway, so I excuse myself to the ladies' room. I note that the seat is up and figure that's usual; mine aren't the only tits in the bar—or even the nicest—but I think I'm the only one here who sits down to pee. Well, except for Miss Bunny, who is the topic of discussion at the sink when I come out.

"Did you hear what she said to Aunt Titty? She said . . ."

"Honey, don't repeat anything she says. Don't even waste your breath. I swear somebody ought to push that bitch out in traffic."

"Somebody might if she don't watch herself. Look out, baby, Tommy's girlfriend needs to use the sink." For some reason, this makes me feel all tingly, although it might just be delayed effects from the syrup drink. I think it over as I'm washing my hands and realize that it's not the drink, I really do feel tingly, and I realize that I've just been afforded more courtesy and acceptance in this drag queen hooker bar in forty minutes than I've gotten at Boardner's the entire time I've been hanging out there. Night after night, dollar after dollar, beer after beer, at Boardner's I'm just another pair of tits in a bustier that the girls see as competition and the guys see as not quite up to Hollywood par. But here I feel welcome, even liked. That part might actually be the syrup. But it feels good anyway.

I dry my hands and touch up my face, making sure to exchange pleasantries with the "girls"—I figure I'd better stay on their good side—and come out to find that Tommy's already gotten us another round. "I won 'em," he says, and I down mine while punching up another set of Patsy Cline on the jukebox. It occurs to me that I am

171

getting more free drinks here than I get at Boardner's, and nobody is trying to sleep with me—well, nobody except Tommy, and he isn't trying that hard.

On any given night, he's as likely to choose dope as he is to choose me. Those are the nights that Raelynn and I creep around our old haunts, trolling for hair gods and wondering what we'll do when the workers' comp place finally closes down. I decide that I'll bring Raelynn here with me next time, then think better of it. I know myself well enough to know that a lot of the things that make me feel happy and cozy tend to make other people feel squeamish and uncomfortable. This is probably one of those things.

Speaking of feeling strange, between the free beers and the mystery shot, I'm starting to feel a little odd myself. I round Tommy up and we head back to our building, stumbling up the stairs together for the usual foggy post-bar sex and pass out. Tonight, instead of rolling over and passing out, Tommy props himself up on a pillow and says, in a remarkably lucid tone, "There's something I probably ought to tell you."

I brace myself for the inevitable horrible news. Nobody has ever started off any good news with that line. He's already told me he's a junkie, so that's out; and I know he doesn't have a job, so that's out too. I guess most logical people would assume that he was about to admit to having some dreaded disease, which needless to say has entered my mind more than once since our association began, but because the evening's scenes are still flashing fresh in my mind, there's only one thing I can think of, and I immediately assume it to be true.

"You're a transvestite prostitute," I say mournfully. I always thought his legs were too smooth to be natural.

Tommy laughs so loudly the asshole next door bangs on the wall until Tommy hurls a combat boot back.

"No. I'm not a transvestite prostitute," he says, and then gets serious again. "Do you know Tina?" I shake my head, and Tommy points at the wall where he just threw my boot. "She lives two doors down from you in the back apartment. The Filipina chick."

"You mean the stripper?" There is one Asian girl— well, a woman actually, no spring chicken—who I sometimes see leaving dressed as a sexy cop, or nurse, or even, at Christmas, Mrs. Claus. She has pitted skin and cold eyes; Raelynn calls her Noriega and insists that the guns she packs in her sexy cop holsters are real.

"Well, she does strip-o-grams, but she's actually an actress." Tommy pauses. "She's my, well, we kind of date."

"When?" I can't figure out the logistics on this one, since for the better part of a week he's been in my apartment.

"She's been out of town for two weeks," he sighs, "visiting her sister. But she's coming back tomorrow."

I sigh, too. I should have known this was too good to last.

Q: *You've got to be shitting me. You're being ironic, right?*

A: *Don't forget . . . he lives right downstairs. Convenience makes up for a lot in my book.*

"So how long have you two been dating?" I'm hopeful that we can continue what we've got going on. Maybe I can usurp her if they are just casually dating.

"About three and a half years."

Shit.

Before I can make a counter offer, the phone rings. As I've been doing ever since the screenplay debacle, I let the machine pick up so I can see who it is. It's Raelynn. I'll call her back; I want to wail to her about Tommy's bombshell, but I can't with him here.

"Hey, Anne. Raelynn. I know you're probably still out with that nasty boy downstairs . . ."

"Hey!" Tommy looks indignant. I snap up the receiver and tell her I'll call her back, then turn to Tommy.

"You probably ought to go downstairs."

"Why?"

"Um, I don't know." *Maybe because you have a girlfriend? Maybe because you've been stringing me along for free drinks for two weeks? Maybe because I feel like an idiot and not for the first time this month?* "I just think you should is all."

"But this is probably the last night that I'll actually get to spend the whole night here," he complains. "I mean, I still want to see you. That's not going to change. We just have to be discreet."

You would have to be pretty damn discreet, by my estimation, for your girlfriend to not find out you were seeing the girl two apartments over. And I don't know if Tommy has it in him. He's usually pretty loaded, which doesn't make him the picture of discretion. Still, I have to admit, I want to keep seeing him. Time for another sigh.

"OK, look. Go downstairs for about a half an hour and then you can come back up and spend the night. I just need to take care of some stuff." I need to call Raelynn and debrief, I need to take a Valium, and I need to listen to sad songs about being the Other Woman, not necessarily in that order. Once I take care of all of that, I'll welcome Tommy back, against Raelynn's advice and my better judgment.

7

There Goes the Neighborhood
The Smell of Hairspray Gives Way to Teen Spirit

ey, guess what? I'm the next lucky winner," Rae-lynn says as she passes my desk on the way out of Andrew's office. Andrew follows her at a respectful distance as she goes to clean out her desk. He refuses to meet my eyes as I stare in disbelief at the person who just fired my best friend. The ongoing job cuts are not Andrew's fault, and the order in which they're being carried out isn't his doing either, but nowadays he eats lunch alone. It's like he has the stink of death on him, and no one wants to go to Del Taco with the Grim Reaper. I feel sorry for him, but pissed off at the same time. He's my friend, too, but he's also the Man, or at least the hatchet man. And now, with Raelynn gone and Andrew as good as gone, I'm going to be spending a lot of lonely lunch breaks at Del Taco myself.

"It's not a big deal," Raelynn says that night, over drinks at Boardner's. "It's not like it was a career. It was just a job. And besides," she adds, twirling her lemon wedge in her gin and tonic, "I've been thinking of moving to Texas, anyway. I hear Austin is cool."

"*Texas?*" I can't believe Raelynn would leave me here alone. Outside of Tommy, who I now can only see a couple of nights a week, she's my only companion—my partner in crime, shoulder to cry on, and never ending font of calming blue pills. I can't imagine what I'm going to do without her. "Why not just look for another job? It's a big city. You could probably find a *better* job!" I try hard to sound encouraging, but Raelynn is decisive.

"Nah, it's not just the job. I've been thinking about it for a while. You will, too," she adds, downing the rest of her drink. "It's not the same here anymore. You see it happening, don't you? It's all changing."

I don't answer but she knows that I see it. I see what she's talking about every time I venture back out to the Strip, which is less and less often these days—truth be told, for the past few months I've spent a lot more time at the Blacklite than anywhere else. When I made the decision to come out to Los Angeles, spur of the moment though it was, there were some factors that were key in convincing me. First and foremost was Hollywood's position as the Mecca of metal. I came out here because I wanted to be where metal was happening, and when I got here, I was not disappointed. From Boardner's to the Strip, the city was crawling with metal bands who needed reviews, publicity, press kits, and girlfriends. For a year and a half, I was in high cotton, if in no other way, at least where metal was concerned. But that first Palladium show, the one where I almost bought it, was a harbinger of what was to come. Alice in Chains, Soundgarden, Pearl Jam, and their Seattle ilk are taking over the airwaves and the newsstands, clad in grubby flannel and drab thermals, leaving the lingering hair gods out in the cold with nothing but their fringed suede jackets and skintight pants to keep them warm.

With the influx of grunge bands, our roster at Around the World is down by half. The new bands come in with publicists from Seattle and established followings of their own. They don't come to Hollywood green, like the hair bands did. Some of the local bands who haven't hit yet try weakly to get with the program, trading their long hair for goatees and dressing down to look the part, but that doesn't help us—when you're trying to establish yourself as a grunge band, the last person you want in charge of your image is some broad who looks like a leftover extra from a Great White video.

"Yeah, I know," I say glumly. "I don't know what I'm gonna do when this place closes. I feel like I should be trying to do more music stuff, but I just can't get excited about these new bands." The only band we currently have on our roster that is even showing a hint of making it through the hair metal shakeout is Ku De Tah, and they do the funk-metal bass-slappy stuff that drove me crazy when I first got here but now doesn't seem so bad compared to everything else. I do most of the work on their account, since Renee won't touch anything that smells of rap, but so far all of their contact info has her name on it. I haven't brought it up with Morgan and Heather because I know they'll just blow sunshine up my ass about tours that are never going to happen, and besides, Raelynn is right. I feel the change coming, and I know that I am not long for Around the World or Los Angeles either. I just don't know where I'm supposed to go from here.

"I hear Austin has a pretty good music scene."

"Yeah, right. Honky-tonks and hoedowns aren't my style, but thanks anyway." I'm just trying to cover up my hurt feelings, and Raelynn knows it, so she doesn't take offense.

Instead she slides me two Valiums and orders us another round. I don't know what I'm gonna do without her.

Q: *So obviously you were completely unaware that Austin was already well on its way to being the next important music scene.*

A: *Not totally—South by Southwest had been taking place for four years at that point, and of course I'd heard about that, but most of what was coming out of Austin then was a little too close to Athens-style alternative for my taste: too clever, too smug, and not nearly grimy enough to be compelling. In short, the difference between a feed-shop trucker hat and a boutique trucker hat is kind of like the difference between a Mexican poncho and a Sears poncho, with all nods to Frank Zappa.*

So let's recap. I am not writing for any magazines. I am barely doing any publicity. I am not making any new connections in music journalism, and I am not meeting any influential persons in the music industry. I am, however, spending a lot of time in a drag queen hooker bar, processing a lot of bogus workers' compensation claims, and having an affair with an unemployed junkie behind the back of an aging stripper. Just in case you thought this wasn't all working out famously, you know.

✠

With Tommy being less available, I've gotten his permission to take my other gentlemen friends—and I use the terms *gentlemen* and *friends* very loosely—to the Blacklite on the nights

he is with Tina. Since Tina doesn't drink, there's no chance
Tommy and I will ever run into each other there with other
people, not that that really matters but it's something I want
to avoid. As Raelynn pointed out when I finally decided it was
time to introduce her to the Blacklite, unless you're looking
for a drag queen hooker, there is really only one reason to go
to the Blacklite, and that is to get hammered. I would dispute
that; in fact, I would say that I go for the ambience, and the
camaraderie, and for the eclectic jukebox that I've grown to
love. (Bar-Kays, anyone?) The men from the Saint Francis
Mission across the street don't seem interested in any of these
things, but they're another one of the things that keeps me
coming back. Why? Because when they're looking to buy a
lady a drink, until they reach that magical point of inebriation
where they can't tell the difference anymore, I'm the only
lady there.

That's mainly a concern on the nights I come to the
Blacklite alone or with Raelynn—since getting laid off, she's
consented to come along a few times, but usually not, as
Raelynn is not nearly as enamored with the Blacklite as I am.
Most nights I bring male company, the vestigial hair gods
I find on the Strip and at Boardner's, still proudly tossing
their tresses and polishing their licks, not yet comprehending
that the hair-metal boat sailed months ago and they weren't
on it. I bring them to the Blacklite . . . out of meanness.
Pure, simple meanness.

Like Kelsey Grammer at Boardner's last year, a part
of me will always be the eighth-grader who got picked last
in gym class. More specifically, I was the girl who sat out
couples skate at Golden Skateworld while my friends sped

181

around the rink with pimply-faced boys who snuck cigarettes behind the building and carried smuggled airline bottles of vodka in the tops of their tube socks. At Golden Skateworld, as I sat alone on the upholstered benches while Foreigner's "Cold as Ice" played over the crackling loudspeakers, I told myself that it didn't matter because I was brainy and talented and those boys were dumb as dirt and going nowhere. They might look like Matt Dillon and my friends might go all moony-eyed for their kisses, but they didn't have a brain among them and that made me *better*.

I told myself that again in high school, when I didn't get a sideways glance from the punk rock guys in the bands that the Open High kids flocked to see. I made fun of their malaprops and acted as if their slack-jawed Marlon Brando rebellion didn't make me ache with longing. I honed my sarcasm in the coffeeshop with D&D-playing guys who were moony-eyed over *me,* something I pretended not to notice because I didn't like them *like that.* The cool guys were always the butt of our running sour grape commentary, pointed observations about their shallowness and low intelligence. Yes, I see the irony . . . now. As a teenager, I thought I was the picture of depth, as did most of my fellow coffeeshop denizens.

Q: *What is it about coffeeshops that draws self-important assholes with delusions of enlightenment?*

A: *Ummmmm . . . the scones?*

Pity the poor would-be hair gods who have to pay penance for my teenaged slights. Completely ignorant that they are going to pay for crimes they did not commit, they ask me out and suffer for their foolhardiness. I bring them to the Black-lite to see if they will squirm, and if they do, woe be unto them, because when it comes to making verbal mincemeat of good-looking-but-not-very-bright men, spurned nerd girls are *nothing* compared to drag queen hookers.

"*Oh,* Annie, this one can read," says Carmella with mock astonishment when my newest plaything, a strapping blue-haired Bangladeshi drummer named Arafat Kazi, recites the drink specials. The girls are charmed by his accent, educated as he was in posh post-colonial British schools, and I am impressed by his ability to cite Arthur Conan Doyle and Bruce Dickinson in the same breath. In fact, it's how we met—standing outside of Boardner's one night, waiting to find out where to go for the inevitable after party, I thought I heard someone over my shoulder quoting Poe . . . and when I say quoting Poe, I don't mean squawking "Nevermore" or some other such tripe that any idiot with a tenth-grade edu-cation or a working knowledge of *The Simpsons* could quote. I mean an entire stanza of one of Poe's less-lauded poems, recited in the accent that will later charm the Blacklite "girls," making it just that much more compelling and lyrical to my drunken ears. The fact that the poem is "To Annie" easily passes as kismet at three A.M., and I am more than willing to stagger off down Cherokee Avenue to Arafat's basement apartment, leaving the after parties for another night. His bookshelf rivals my own back in Richmond, a little heavier on the British literature, but he has an excuse, and having someone actually get my literary references for the first time in months is refreshing and challenging. Unfortunately, it's probably also his undoing. "You wastin' your time with her," Carmella says, stroking his massive thigh. "She likes the *stupid* ones." She's right, as terrible as it sounds, and though Arafat is probably the most formidable opponent I have found yet, he'll be nothing more than an exotic tryst for me, largely because I can't verbally bat him around like a dimwitted ball of twine.

He is a sport, though, sticking around long enough to see a catfight that moves from the bathroom to the barroom to the street and finally ends in broken fingernails, tears, and hugs for two besotted working girls, and a round for the house when they air kiss and make up. We are inseparable for the better part of a month, but like the college-radio people at William and Mary, Arafat's intense devotion to things lofty and literary soon evokes a lowbrow backlash from my anti-intellectual side. I start snapping at his poetry recitations and stop laughing at his ironic asides. I don't like having to think so much when I'm trying to have a good time, and I especially don't like it when he tries to engage me in egghead banter in public. There's a reason I left my Norton anthology at home. Doesn't he know he's blowing my cover? I finally have to give him the "It's not you, it's me" talk, which he takes with all of the dignity and grace of a heavy metal drummer who was raised by a cadre of servants and housemen. Even after we're no longer an item, I know I can always call Arafat for mid-morning jaunts to shoot the shit over Grand Slams at the rock 'n' roll Denny's and get quick answers to my nagging "who wrote that poem that goes . . ." questions when nobody's listening, like when I am sneaking a go at the *New York Times* crossword in my apartment, with the shades drawn—and occasionally I kick myself for whatever glitch in my programming that yearns for a bonehead beau.

My next contestant doesn't fare nearly as well at the Blacklite, where the girls are still a little bitter over Arafat's absence and don't hesitate to let me know.

"Annie, Annie," sighs Brandi as she runs her fingers through the glossy curls of my next victim. "This one isn't nearly as cute as the last one. What's your name, baby?" Baby ain't saying; instead he storms out of the bar, issuing a barrage of profanity, presumably to walk home since, as usual, I'm driving. This is all perfectly hilarious to me, Billy, and the girls at the Blacklite, and we all have a round on the house and replay the events leading up to his departure again and again. That one I was a little sorry to see go; he was tough-guy good-looking, and I'd barely even gotten a chance to talk to him before Brandi scared him off. I tell myself that he was probably sour, anyway, and serenade Brandi with a resounding chorus of "her" song on the jukebox —*Brandy, you're a fine girl, what a good wife you would be*—because she's better company anyway, and definitely better dressed.

✙

One night, back at Boardner's on Raelynn's insistence ("I just can't deal with the Blacklite tonight; I'm tired of hanging out with men who have nicer tits than I do"), I give my number to Steve Stavros, the guitarist for the Seen, a local funk-rock knockoff group with the same slappy-bass solos and homeboy rap interludes as all of the other local funk-rock knockoff groups. Lately, any band that isn't trying to be Pearl Jam is trying to be the Red Hot Chili Peppers, and it's all wearing just a little thin with me. I give him my number in spite of my misgivings, though, because I've gone out with guys who have done a lot worse than rip off Parliament, and besides, he's kind of cute. We go out on a couple of dates, real dates, that he actually pays for—movies, dinner, drinks, the works. I've almost forgotten what a real date was like. I go along to a couple of parties to see his band play, the first time since Richmond that I've been "with the band" in the Pamela Des Barres sense. I'd almost forgotten how heady it was, even when the band isn't exactly what you'd pick if you had your choice. Just watching him on stage, and looking through the crowd at the girls eyeing him, a lot of them better looking than me, makes me feel like the fucking prom queen for once in my life. We don't have much to talk about, and his looks are more Charlie Watts than Keith Richards, but as long as I recharge my prom queen batteries by seeing him on stage every couple of weeks, I'm happy. I don't take him to the Blacklite, largely because I know that, in the eyes of the girls, the last one was cuter and they won't hesitate to say so.

Aside from the adoring fans and the glory they shine on Steve in my eyes, the other great thing about hanging out with him is that he is the first guy since Tommy who can keep up with my ever-increasing alcohol consumption. Steve can put away a whole fifth of liquor—and, unlike Tommy, he'll actually buy it himself—and still be ready to head for the next party, which makes him the perfect companion for the newly fortified me, the me who is doing a better job of looking like Lester Bangs than writing like him. What started out as a way for me to swallow my pride and be the hack I

needed to be to make it out here is turning into an excuse
not to write, a reason to turn down freelance work in favor
of drinking in dives with Steve—or sometimes at the Blacklite, alone. At least nobody at the Blacklite is asking me to sell
out my artistic integrity for a half-page three-color ad.

Partly to try and make up for the Tommy days, I set
Raelynn up with Nick, the Seen's slappy-slap bass player.
After one date he gets picked up on outstanding traffic war-
rants and ends up cooling his heels in the Los Angeles
County Jail. Try as I might to get her to visit—"he's lonely,
and besides, you can't move to Texas without ever seeing the
inside of the jail"—she chooses instead to wait until he gets
out to resume their courtship. Fortunately for all involved—
the Seen, Raelynn, and especially Nick—he only has to pull
thirty days, and we pick him up at the end of his stay in my
trusty Hyundai, singing off-key renditions of "Thirty Days in
the Hole" on the way. We take him straight to Steve's house
to brush up on his bass-slapping, because the Seen is going to
be opening for Trulio Disgracias at Al's Bar on Saturday. They
sound like another Red Kennedys–style joke band, but in
fact, Trulio is a side project for members of Fishbone and the
original bass slappers, Parliament Funkadelic. This is a huge
deal for the Seen, and I've even promised to come out of
retirement and write a review of their set for *Screamer*. Just
when you think Fortuna has spun you downward, things
start looking up again.

Unfortunately, what goes up must come down, and the
fall is often a complete surprise. Saturday night, as Raelynn
and I drink a sloppy draft-beer toast to good times and bad
boys between sets at Al's Bar, we have no idea that the wheel

is already in motion a few feet away from where we sit, starting its descent once again. As far as we know, the night is going swimmingly. In fact, we are practically gloating at our current position, on the guest list, with the band, as it were. No, folks, it doesn't get much better than this, and here we are living the dream. That is, until Vic the Mouth, the band's diminutive lead singer, makes his way down from the dressing room and offers to buy our next round. Suspicious. Suspicious indeed.

"Uh, Anne?" Shuffle, shuffle. Gulp of beer. Earring tug.

"Yeah, Vic?"

"I think you're really cool." Nervous hair toss. Goatee scratch, shuffle, gulp.

"Thanks, Vic."

"And no matter what happens between you and Steve, I hope we can still be friends." That whirring sound you hear is the wheel spinning downward. Raelynn gives me the stink-eye, but I don't even wait for her signal. I am already halfway up the rickety stairway/fire escape that leads to the dressing room, adrenaline rushing and a mixture of morbid curiosity and dread building in my chest. I'm not sure what I'm going to find, but I'm pretty sure my night is about to get a lot more interesting and a lot less great.

Upstairs in the dressing room, the members of Trulio Disgracias, their girlfriends, and the rest of the Seen are crowded onto two couches, drinking, smoking, and generally doing what bands do backstage, which is actually sit around and wait a lot. This is one of the many myths that have been shattered for me since my *CREEM*-reading days: the myth of what happens backstage. Now having been backstage more times than I care to count, I can say with some authority that the backstage experience resembles nothing so much as an airport waiting room.

Apparently, though, my date feels the need to live up to the hype. Seated on a folding chair by the door, Steve is displaying the dexterity that makes him such a good guitarist by managing to seamlessly alternate sips of beer, drags of his cigarette, and tongue-wrestling a busty blonde in a Daisy Mae gingham halter who is giving him a music-free lap dance in front of God, Blackbird McKnight, and everybody.

"Hey!" Steve grabs my hand without letting go of the blonde's waist. It seems like everyone in the room has stopped to see what's going to happen, which means I am now not only being humiliated and cheated on, but I am being humiliated and cheated on in front of a roomful of famous and semifamous musicians.

"You suck," I say unoriginally and try to pull my hand away. Steve hangs on even as he takes another swig of his beer.

"Hey, babe, don't be mad," he says, rivaling me for lack of creativity in the face of confrontation. I wrest my hand away and grab Raelynn's arm.

"Come on, we're going," I say, not willing to provide any more entertainment for the voyeuristic dressing room crew.

"Aw, don't go," Steve says unconvincingly as the blonde rests her head on his shoulder. "Don't go," he says again, without getting up. Raelynn and I clamber down the stairs and straight out the door.

I drive home in a blind rage. Raelynn tries to talk me into going to Boardner's, but I think I would clock any musician who tried to talk to me, just on principal. As a show of solidarity, she vows never to see Nick again. Not that it's a big deal for her; she was mainly dating him because of Steve and me anyway. With her plans to move to Austin solidifying faster than I would like to see, getting attached to a bass-slapping pretty boy is definitely not on her agenda—though I can't say it didn't occur to me that if they hit it off she might change her mind about moving. (I'm a good friend, but I have to think about my needs, too.) I drop her off at her apartment and go home to mine, where the phone is ringing when I walk in the door.

"Hello?"

"Hey, does this mean you're not going to write our review?" It doesn't seem to occur to him that I am the last person he wants discussing him in print right now. I drop a hint.

"Well, I don't know. I might still write it, but I ought to warn you, I'm not feeling particularly magnanimous right about now."

Pause.

"What does that mean?"

Q: *So did you end up writing the review?*

A: *Actually, I did. I gave them a pretty good review, with a lot of praise for Vic's singing, Nick's bass slapping, and Darryl's drumming. In fact, the lackluster guitar playing was the only real weak spot. . . .*

Q: *So you did exactly what you complained that journalists are unfairly accused of doing.*

A: *Hey, even a broken clock is right twice a day. Besides, he really wasn't a very good guitarist, scout's honor. The spurning was a blessing in disguise for my journalistic integrity. I swear.*

✠

With Steve and Nick out of our lives and Raelynn's departure coming in less than a month, we return to Boardner's with a vengeance. We're there almost every night, and after parties are the order of the day—or night, as the case may be. One such night finds us slouched on the couch of an unknown stranger, nursing warm beers at four A.M., hoping to make our meager stash last until six when we can buy more. While we wait, we amuse ourselves by watching two good ol' boys of the hair-metal variety, both as drunk if not drunker than we are, repeatedly high-five each other while screaming "BILL CLINTON! *Yeeeeeeee-haw!*"

"Who is Bill Clinton?" I slur, more wondering aloud than actually expecting an answer.

"He's the governor of Arkansas," Raelynn says bemusedly. Trust an Okie to know, but what does that have to do with the price of beer in Hollywood?

"Why do they keep screaming his name like that?"

"I dunno." Raelynn rustles in the empty cardboard carton, hoping in vain to find a magically appearing cold one. Needless to say, she doesn't. "Hey, guys," she says, flinging the empty box at them, "enough with the Bill Clinton already! You're in California now."

"And so will Bill Clinton be, too, when he's president of *all fifty fuckin' states!*" howls the spokesman for the two,

191

then they let loose with another *yeee-haw* and high-five each other again.

"Bill Clinton for President," the second one cheers. "He fuckin' *rocks*!"

"Whatever, dude," Raelynn says, shaking her head. She laughs. "He's kind of a horndog."

"We know!" They high-five each other again. "Horndog in the White House! *Yeee-haw*!" Raelynn isn't buying it. "He hasn't got a chance. He won't even get nominated."

I don't know from Bill Clinton. All I know is we have almost two hours until we can get more beer and I'm starting to feel like just going to sleep instead—and apparently I'm not the only one.

"What the *fuck,* man? It's *foo-ah* in the morning!" Mike Gasper storms into the living room in boxers and a bed-head, surveying the scene in what is apparently his apartment.

"Chill, dude, just havin' a few people over," the unknown host, who may or may not be Mike Gasper's roommate explains.

"Well, keep it down! People are tryin' to sleep heah," he grumbles. I guess even conservative rockers need to rest sometimes.

"Hey!" This from one of the Arkansas boys, who obviously are unfamiliar with Gasper's leanings. Raelynn and I exchange a worried look, both apparently thinking the same thing—*horndog or no, Bill Clinton had better be a Republican or things are gonna get ugly*—right as the oblivious duo screams in unison:

"BILL CLINTON FOR PRESIDENT! *Yeeeeeee—*"

"OK, that does it! EVERYBODY OUT!" That answers that question.

I've been to a lot of parties, and I've gotten kicked out for a lot of reasons, but this is the first time I've ever seen a party called on account of Bill Clinton—although I'll bet he's been kicked out of his share.

✝

I suppose the next plot twist needs a setup. Unfortunately, I have none. What's missing from this story is the detail about how Red got my phone number. This should, in fact, be a fairly significant plot point, as getting him, his number, or even his name was a longstanding and elusive goal of Rae-lynn's and mine and has been referred to more than once heretofore. Suffice to say that the detail about the information exchange is lost to time and too many dollar drafts. I am assuming that the transfer took place at Boardner's, since we never saw him off-duty, and I am also assuming that I gave him my number with no bidding from anyone other than Raelynn and good old Jack Daniels. In fact, even though I have no recollection of any of this, I'd be fairly willing to bet that the details are similar to what I've just told you. It's remarkable how predictable my life had become at this point. What I can tell you with certainty is that he called me one night after midnight, collect, from the Los Angeles County Jail and, in a fit of unmitigated idiocy, I accepted the charges.

Ask me now what he was in for. I couldn't tell you that either. What I can tell you is that the following Saturday I find myself in line at visiting time, wondering mirthlessly how I

came to be in a queue where I seem to be the only one without a tattoo on my face. At least the praying hands on the
neck of the man in front of me give me something interesting
to look at as the slow-moving line inches its way toward the
door. I wait patiently for my turn at the window, where
I am given a slip of paper with Red's full name—Dwight
MacPherson—and the number of a visiting cubicle. Then I sit
down and wait. It occurs to me that I should have brought a
book, or a crossword puzzle, but then I realize that would
make me look even more out of place than I already am, as if
that were possible between my Mister Peabody glasses and
lack of facial tattoos. I try to act casual while I wait my turn,
and I also try not to stare at my fellow visitors too much,
intrigued though I am.

When they call my number, I stand up with thirty or so
of the other visitors and head into a catacomb of cubicles,
each with a beat-up telephone receiver and a window through
which you can see your orange-jumpsuited loved one. I follow the arrows to my cubicle, E-7, and find it already occu-
pied by a tall, skinny woman with dark brown skin and an
elaborate purple hairdo. Just to make sure, I peek through her
window and see a black man remarkable for his lack of flowing red curls.

"That isn't him," I say out loud.

"It *better* not be him," the woman says to me, swiveling
her head like a cobra. I back my nerdy little ass up in a hurry,
but her inmate is more understanding, shouting through the
glass, "White boy? He down the end!"

I head to the end of the row, buffeted by more helpful
prisoners who continue to point me in the direction of

Dwight, apparently the only white boy in the Los Angeles County Jail. By the time I get to the end of the row, he's gone looking for me on the next aisle, and we keep chasing each other, aided by pointed fingers and shouted directions, all accompanied by the repeated question "White boy? White boy? White boy?" I finally find him on a far aisle, in a booth that's missing its receiver, so there's really only so much we can communicate. He shouts his thanks at me for coming, and I shout back "what happened?" but he either can't hear me or pretends that he can't. We're hopelessly pantomiming questions—I don't even attempt to spell anything in American Sign Language—when the bell rings and the visitors are herded out to make way for the next group.

Over the course of the next couple of weeks, I accept more collect calls from Dwight, never finding out what he's in for or how he got my number, but being reminded with every call that he's lost his job and his apartment because he got arrested and he's going to need a place to stay when he gets out.

Raelynn takes me by both shoulders and looks me square in the face. "Are you sure you want to do this?"

"Well, I can't just leave him to rot on the street!" Shades of Andy, my high school boyfriend. I don't know who made me the ASPCA of girlfriends, but I do a damn fine job of it. In this case, there is a little bit of the prom queen wannabe at work, because after almost two years of ogling him at Boardner's and romanticizing him with Raelynn in our Winchell's debriefings after the bars closed, the thought that he could, after all this time, be mine is an ego boost for sure. He is gorgeous, all jawline and shoulders and glossy red mane.

And from what he's been telling me on the phone, he's in a band, and they have an agent and a demo, and as soon as he gets out they're supposed to do a showcase, though I haven't been able to ascertain for whom. But above all of the selfish reasons, the ones that boost my ego and fuel my fantasies of showing everyone that I've got what it takes to snag a hair god, the real reason is the ever-compelling sense of duty and responsibility I feel to rescue him from himself. *Give me your tired, your poor, your incarcerated hair gods yearning to breathe free!* "I can't turn my back on him when he needs help."

"Sure you can. You don't even know him!" Raelynn, as usual, brings the harsh light of reason to the discussion, something I choose to ignore when left to my own devices.

"But he's counting on me. And besides," I say, trying to convince myself as well as Raelynn, "It will be worth it in ambience alone to have someone that good-looking hanging around the apartment! I mean, you have to admit he's gorgeous."

"Gorgeous doesn't pay the rent," says party-pooper Raelynn. "And besides, I know you. You're going to get tired of him. And your apartment is really, really small." That is a concern—the apartment, I mean. But I'm considering this arrangement to be temporary, just until he gets on his feet.

"How do you know he's going to get on his feet? Have you guys set a deadline for how long he has to get a job?"

"I'll talk to him about it," I say, just to get her off my back. I don't tell her that part of the reason I'm so hesitant to let go of him is that with her moving to Austin, I'm worried that I won't have anyone but half of Tommy. One whole jobless boyfriend beats half a jobless boyfriend is what I'm thinking. I don't say so, though, because I know she'll find some stupid way to make it seem like a bad deal—as far-fetched as that may seem. And I start rearranging my things to make room for Dwight.

✠

"So where did he say he was from?" Still not thrilled with the arrangement, Raelynn asks way too many questions about Dwight now that he's moved in.

"Kankakee, Illinois," I say for the third time. I think she just likes the sound of it. We're at the Blacklite, where I absolutely will not bring Dwight. I told him we were going shopping.

"Damn. And I thought Bixby was white trash. If you have his babies, they're gonna have rattails and dirty feet from the day they're born," she warns.

"And they'll walk around in saggy diapers and nothing else," I add. "And I'll put purple Kool-Aid in their bottles."

"The older ones will eat bologna and white bread sand-wiches for breakfast . . ."

"And bring 'em to me in the kitchen and say 'put some more *may*'naisse on it, Momma!'" We are both having way too much fun with this.

"And you'll be wearing terrycloth shorts and a tube top . . ."

"And smoking a Misty Menthol! And I'll scream 'Damn it, Junior, cain't you see Momma's doin' a seek an' find puzzle?'" We dissolve in helpless peals of laughter while the drag queens shake their heads at the two silly white chicks.

To be honest, I'm laughing because I don't know what else

to do. I haven't shared all of the unpleasant details with anyone, not even Raelynn, mainly because I know she's going to say she told me so and she's absolutely right. The situation with Dwight goes beyond not having a job. It goes far beyond that.

✛

The first night after I picked him up at the jail was all right. He talked a lot on the ride home. An awful lot. So much that the words poured out on top of one another, sometimes not quite matching up into whole sentences. That was OK, though, because I figured he hadn't had anybody to talk to for a good long while. We dropped his stuff off at my apartment and went to Boardner's, where Dwight didn't get the hearty welcome back that I was expecting from his former coworkers. Instead, they looked at us worriedly as we holed up in a back booth, alone. Dwight had a bottle of Tussinex he'd been prescribed by the prison infirmary, and he poured liberal shots of it into our Jack and Cokes. This slowed his patter down to a dull roar. I toured him around town like a new convertible, to all the bars until they closed and then to the after party. I felt vindicated. *I may not have plastic breasts or silicone lips, but hey now, look at the arm candy! Say it with me: "I am! Somebody!"* We got home and he promptly passed out, which was fine by me because I was exhausted just from listening to him talk.

The next day was worse. He was already talking when I woke up, to no one in particular. He was pacing around my tiny apartment, digging through his bag of stuff and tossing his gorgeous hair around furiously. I could pick out little bits and pieces of what he was saying. "They don't know who they're messing with . . . want me to run for office? I ain't your fool . . . that ain't in the Constitution . . . get me a lawyer . . . show them who's boss." I got a cup of coffee and watched him, rapt and horrified, for about an hour. It was like I wasn't even there. Stacey called, and after my efforts to pass him off as the television finally failed, I told her the truth after swearing her to secrecy. At the time of her call, I still had hopes that things might get better, that maybe we were going through an adjustment period, a post-incarceration debrief. But that was a week ago, and things have gotten worse since then. It's a testament to the seriousness of the situation that I was able to have an entire phone conversation about the depth of his insanity and he didn't even notice, couldn't even hear me over his own constant string of paranoid ramblings.

Once I determine that the situation isn't going to change and that, in fact, he is batshit crazy, I give up on encouraging him to look for work. Instead, I start encouraging him to find somewhere else to stay. He has a little black book full of girls' numbers, and I urge him to call them while I am at work.

"You want me to call other girls?" He looks like he might cry. "I thought you were my *girlfriend*."

What is there to say, really, to something like that? "I'm sorry," I say simply, not delving into the whys or the wherefores because they're things you just don't say to someone. *I'm sorry you turned out to be crazy. I'm sorry you stay up all night laughing and whispering. I'm sorry you wander up and down the hall, muttering and scaring my neighbors.* The building manager has asked me twice when he's leaving, and even Tommy has been checking on me to make sure everything is OK. If I weren't so busy trying to figure out how to extricate myself from the situation, I would be embarrassed. Embarrassment is always the first thing to go.

✠

Finally, I pour out the whole sordid story to Raelynn. She is aghast, but not surprised.

"So what do you want to do?"

"I've got to get him out of there." I'm losing sleep and I'm afraid of losing my lease. "I don't want to throw him out on the street, though, Raelynn. He can't manage."

"But he can't stay with you—*you* can't manage *him*." She's right. The only peace I've had in two weeks is when he's asleep. Then I sit and watch him, his mouth finally still, his gorgeous face and muscled torso belying the madness inside. I watch him sleep and I feel horrible and guilty and mean because this was all a game to me, back when he was just another dumb hair-metal guy I could make fun of with my friends at the Blacklite. Stupid is funny, but crazy is not. I don't want to play this game anymore, but I'm in too deep to quit.

Raelynn and I decide we will give him a week to find somewhere to go, and when the week is up I will change the locks and put his things outside, no ifs, ands, or buts. I don't know if a week is fair and I don't know if he even understands how long that is, but I do know I can't live like this. I go home and tell Dwight the news.

"That's it? Just like that?" I nod. "You're gonna be sorry,

babe, because I'm on my way up!" His eyes are wild as he stuffs clothes back into the garbage bag he came with. "I'm about to have a number one hit. My agent is buying me a Jaguar because he *knows* I'm gonna be huge."

He doesn't have an agent.

"One week," I remind him, and then I leave and go spend the night at Raelynn's.

The last night of Dwight's week happens to coincide with the Widespread Panic and Phish show at the Variety. No fan of Phish but eager to see Dave, who I haven't seen since before I moved to L.A.——thanks to the bad timing of his last West Coast tour coinciding with my visit to Athens—— I'm always up for a Panic show. Dave calls as soon as he gets into town, and we make plans to grab a quick drink before we head for the show. As I gather up a few things for the rest of the evening, I'm stunned to see Dwight watching me with a look of indignant rage.

"Did I just hear you right?"

"It depends," I say, throwing a hairbrush and lipstick into my bag. "What did you hear?"

"Well if I didn't know better, I'd *swear* I just heard my old lady make a *date* with some *rock star RIGHT IN FRONT OF MY FUCKING EYES!*" He slams his fist into the wall.

"OK." I take a deep breath, hoping it will subliminally encourage him to do the same. I keep talking, all the while backing toward the front door. "First of all, it's not a date. I am having a drink with an old friend." Almost to the door, keep talking. Calm, soothing tones. "Second of all, he's not a rock star. He's just a guy in a band that happens to tour." Fudging it, but who's to know? "And third of all, I am not your old lady and I want you out of here when I get back." Technically there are still several hours left until his official deadline, but when you start punching walls, it's time to go.

"You are a cold-hearted woman," he says, his face still to the wall, his fist still resting on the crumbled plaster. Tell me something I don't know. I open the door quietly and slip outside.

In the hall, Tommy is waiting, summoned upstairs by the shaking walls. He doesn't ask me anything but gives me a hug and a beer. I wish he wasn't somebody else's boyfriend just like I wish Dwight wasn't crazy. Wishes aren't horses, though, so I know that no Prince Charming is on the way to spirit me off on his dashing steed. A cold beer from a junkie is better than nothing, and I take it and hope that things will be better when I come home.

✝

"So this is where you hang out now?" Dave is taking in the ambience at the Blacklite serenely; Dave is a Southern gentleman *and* a hippie, and as such, he is pretty laid back about most things, including drag queen hookers. I've missed hanging out with Dave and my Richmond friends; in almost two years I've almost forgotten what it's like not to worry about someone becoming violent, crazy, or just plain mean for no reason at all. Aside from Tommy, all of the guys I know out here are loose cannons, and now I've let the loosest one move into my place.

"Yeah, this is it," I say, kind of proud to have brought him to such a happy, inviting place. Of course, the Quaalude I took backstage at the show is probably making the Blacklite seem a lot more pleasant and comfortable than usual. I'd read all about 'ludes in *CREEM*, but they were taken off the market in the United States in 1984 so I never had the chance to try one until now. What was the FDA thinking? This is great stuff. Everything seems to be moving at about a quarter speed, which is just so much easier to deal with than real life. As an added bonus, it's making the evening—and my time away from Dwight—seem four times as long.

Q: *If Quaaludes are off the market in the United States, where did you get one?*

A: *Ah, the wonders of bands with major label deals and European tours!*

"Oh my God, *Annie*," Carmella howls with dismay. She looks Dave up and down, clutching her rhinestone necklace and shaking her head as she takes in his tie-dyed shirt, moccasins, and shaggy beard. "Annie, Annie, *Annie!*"

Dave smiles benevolently at her, completely and utterly unoffended. I smile too, thinking I'll answer her eventually. It's the same reaction I had to the gaggle of hippie chicks in the bathroom at the show, who took a break from their sink baths to back me into a stall and ask me a million rapid fire questions about Phish because, given my incongruous bustier and leather jacket coupled with my backstage pass, they assumed I was with Elektra.

"Talk to me, Annie!" Carmella cries. "Say something!" I wonder what her hurry is. I'm almost answering her when she throws up her hands in dismay and runs over to Billy in slow motion.

"Annie's over there with *Charles Manson,* and he's put her in some kind of *trance!*"

On any other night, this pronouncement would have me howling with laughter. On Quaalude night, though, as amusing as it is, the best I can manage is a slow grin, spreading across my face, and a languid sip of my beer. Dave's reaction is about the same. Billy looks over at us and shakes his head. There's not much he hasn't seen, working here, and I think he at least has a general idea of what's going on. He knows enough to call us a cab, and I crash for the night at Dave's room at the Hotel Roosevelt, thankful for a respite from Dwight and his rambling.

8

Last Call

L.A. Throws Me the Least Festive Farewell Party Imaginable

by early 1992, Raelynn's prediction seems to be coming true. She's right, things have changed. Of course, she doesn't stick around to see the change happen; the postcard I receive from Austin says her new place is adorable and half the price of her apartment in L.A. After the Dwight debacle, I pretty much stop going to Boardner's or really anywhere but the Blacklite. I'm not without company, though—Tommy has been spending nights at my place once again, in spite of the fact that half of the building is aware of what's going on. I don't relish my position as the other woman, but Tommy is the perfect companion for me at this point, since all I want to do is drink, take pills, and try not to think about the fact that I'll probably be out of a job soon, and then what? With my reasons for being in L.A. vanishing one by one, it's going to be hard for me to justify getting another day job. That is, if I can even find one.

Raelynn's postcard has me thinking about my options, such as they are. I, too, could probably get an apartment— a real apartment, with rooms and stuff—for half the price I'm paying for my slummy little room, provided said apartment was anywhere but Los Angeles. If I'm not writing, why am I shelling out to live in a city this expensive? A year ago I could have argued that it was the music, but that's less true now that grunge has moved in. There are still more good bands here than in Richmond, but that's hardly worth double expenses, to say nothing of the travel cost of going home twice a year to visit.

My dad sees this as a golden opportunity to lure me home. "Now that your little friend moved away, you ought to think about coming home," he says every time I make a lonely call with nothing to say. "You can come back here and go to school."

School. I was so glad to be done with school three short years ago. And for what? To be the next Lester Bangs, to change the face of metal writing and bring back the days when rock magazines had something to say. I thought I was going to take rock 'n' roll journalism by storm. Instead, the only thing I've taken by storm is a dive bar full of men in dresses. My dad doesn't know this, but he does know I'm running out of excuses to stay in L.A. "Why don't you apply to graduate school at VCU and see if you get in?" he says, hoping to trick me into starting to make plans to come home. He's a crafty one, my dad.

"I don't know. I kind of like it here," I say, and I am telling the truth. Fortunately he doesn't ask what it is that I like, because there's no way I could tell him half the stuff, and even if I tried, it would sound preposterous. How do I love thee, Hollywood? Let me count the ways.

I love that I still run into Glenn Danzig at the supermarket occasionally, and when I do, he really does recognize me now, and he reminds me that he keeps my John the Conqueror root on his dresser. I love the dive bars that feel like Bukowski stories come to life—*are* Bukowski stories come to life, where I weave a Bukowski story of my own. I love that my leftover credentials from the music papers can still get me into most of the clubs on the Strip for free, even if I don't want to go as often as I used to. I love that I can walk down to the newsstand on Hollywood Boulevard at any hour of the night and read on the sidewalk to my heart's content, because it's never raining and it's always seventy degrees. I love the Bodhi Tree bookstore, where you can browse everything from Buddhism to Witchcraft and drink free tea while you do it, and the Sisterhood Bookstore where you can buy rude feminist stickers and nag champa incense with your pocket change. I love that the malls are three stories high and the clothes are months, sometimes years, ahead of anything Richmond sees in its paltry one-story malls. I love being able to break bad without feeling like I'm ruining anyone's good name. I love the drag queen hookers and their smart-mouthed comments, and I love Billy the bartender who lets me keep drinking even after the front door locks at two. I love the heavy metal radio station with the morning show slogan "It's hard when you wake up," just because that would never fly in stodgy old Richmond. And maybe love is too strong a word, but I have a deep and abiding affection for my convenient downstairs sometime junkie boyfriend, who sneaks me soup when I'm sick, gets in bar fights to defend my honor (or the shred I have left, anyway), and spends stolen evenings nodding out in front of the television with me on my crappy little futon. It's no rock-star waterbed, but it's home.

When the application for the VCU Creative Writing program arrives completely unbidden, along with a cheery
Mary Engelbreit card from my mom, I stick it under a pile
of Guns N' Roses CDs and forget about it until right
before the deadline. When she calls and asks me how my
application is coming, I lie and say fine, then spend a frantic
three days holed up in the apartment creating a portfolio
of short stories, fueled by beer and tacos delivered by
Tommy. Not that I think I will ever get in, and not that I
really have given the whole idea much thought. More than
anything, I am buying some more time to figure out what
I'm going to do with my life without my parents bugging
me to come home. At least this way I have a couple of
months where I can say I am "waiting to hear something"
and that will keep them off my case. The stories are little
more than a diary of the past few months, all drugs and
hookers and bar fights, sparing none of the tawdry details.
Toward the end of the second day I convince myself I'm
channeling Bukowski, but I know deep down that this is not
the case; I'm just writing sloppy first-person stories from
the point of view of a messed-up rocker chick who drinks
too much. No poetry here.

I mail the stories off and don't think any more of it; I
know that once they get a load of my mediocre transcripts
and my non-academic resume since I left school, it'll be all
over. I feel sorry for my parents even thinking I have a
chance. Their little girl is not the academic type, sad but
true. When I was in high school, though, I took a creative
writing class from a man who was. He favored poems that
described elderly homeless people in wincing detail and

begged to be read in a chest-thumping chant. "You are a *writer*," he would say solemnly to the students who penned such poems. "Even if you never wrote another word in your life, you would *still* be a writer." His eyes would gleam moistly at them as he let the weight of his weighty, weighty words sink in.

At no time did he ever declare me to be a writer. In fact, my smart-ass rock 'n' roll short stories left him so cold that he made a special request that I take no further classes from him during my tenure at Open High School. Not that I was chomping at the bit, anyway. I sharpened my pen in the *other* creative writing class Open High offered, where a gruff newspaper sportswriter slashed us all democratically with a red pen—"trite!" "hackneyed!" "where's your voice?" He pulled no punches and had no favorites. I made As in his class, but there's a wide divide between the copy desk and the ivory tower. I know I'm not cut out for higher learning, not with literary idols who OD on cold medicine and Darvon. They'll sniff me out for sure.

So what am I supposed to do with my life while I wait to hear from VCU? Since everybody else at work seems to have a screenplay stashed away on a floppy disk, I start my own. I figure it can't be any worse than *Fresh Moves*, and somebody paid for *that*. I title my screenplay *Low Rent*. It's about Tommy and Tina and the Blacklite and, in a cameo appearance as the poor misunderstood girl with no future, me. Hemingway said "write what you know," and at this point I don't know much else. In a somewhat overwrought but nonetheless gripping act of sublimation, I have Tommy get creamed by a truck on the way to Mister Kim's Liquor

Store in the final scene. The closing frame is his trademark red and gold Olde English 800 tallboy can, crushed on the pavement, pouring out into the street.

Q: *Wow, that's subtle.*

A: *Hey, I didn't go to film school, OK?*

Writing a screenplay is easier than anything I've ever written, which makes The Idol's failure to cough up the second half of his even more pathetic in retrospect. I don't have to worry about internal dialogue, or describing what the characters look like, or any of the stuff that takes up all of that space in fiction. I don't have anyone breathing down my neck to be nice like I do in journalism. Unfortunately, there's also no room for the snarky observations and smartass Lester Bangsisms that make writing fun for me in the first place. I map out the plot on index cards, then stash them in a drawer and forget them.

✠

It's a Monday morning in mid-April. I'm editing another workers' compensation report, and I'm having a hard time making sense of the report because we've fired most of our translators and replaced all of our transcriptionists with part-time minimum-wage employees. I'm currently working on a report from a kitchen assistant who was harassed by a baker with a suggestively positioned baguette. *He hang the breads like panes at me shout you like.* I'm puzzling over how to punctuate it so that it makes sense without illegally putting words in the complainant's mouth when I see Andrew standing beside my cubicle.

"Hi, Anne." Andrew has aged a decade in the past few months. He looks miserable.

"Hey." I think of showing him the funny report, for old times' sake, then think better of it. He hasn't had much of a sense of humor lately.

Long pause. Slowly it dawns on me why he's here.

"You want to see me in your office."

Andrew sighs. "I'm sorry."

I get up, switch off my screen and walk with him to his office. I am the next lucky winner.

✝

Now that Tommy and I are both unemployed, it's even harder to be subtle about our association. We're at the Blacklite most evenings from early afternoon until well after they close, doing our best to drink up my severance pay as if I don't have to worry about what I'm going to do for rent money when it runs out. Some nights we barely make it home; on one memorable occasion we only make it as far as Stan's Adult World two doors down from the bar. We pass out in a booth, only waking up to put in quarters when the cashier threatens to throw us out. Tommy still splits his time between Tina and me, and on the nights he's at Tina's I go to the Blacklite alone. One night while I'm obliviously playing pinball with Aunt Titty, Billy has the following fractured exchange with one of the new Mission residents who's wandered in for a nip.

211

"God damn," says the new blood, squinting around the bar. "These women are all *men*!"

"Most of 'em." Billy, polishing his omnipresent highball glass, has had this conversation a million times before.

"Well, how about that one?" He points over to the pinball machine, where I, in jeans and a (surprise) stretchy black top, am showing Aunt Titty, resplendent in a rainbow-striped tube dress, how to score a double bonus ball.

"We've got a fan," Titty tells me, and she and I wave flirtatiously at the newcomer.

"Is he looking at you or me?" I can't see a dratted thing in the Blacklite, even with my big nerd glasses. It's always dark and I'm always drunk.

"I don't know, but I guess we'll find out." Titty blows him a kiss and I shake my boobs at him, then we go back to playing pinball.

Billy looks across the bar and doesn't see me, hidden as I am by Titty's broad frame. He just sees Titty.

"That? That's a man."

"No shit." He whistles low, looking at my all-too-visible cleavage and bountiful booty. "Well, he's had some kinda operation, right?"

"Nope," Billy doesn't even look up from his glass this time. "That's just a plain old man, honey."

For the rest of the night, I drink free while the poor guy stares at my boobs like he's going to cry from sheer confusion. Not until he leaves to make his midnight curfew do we talk to Billy and figure out what happened. Titty thinks it's a lot funnier than I do. I can't say I haven't noticed that over the past few months I've started to look, for lack of a better word, *hard*. My eyes are puffy, my cheeks sallow, and my jaw slack. Of course I can't be one of those women who gets elegantly wasted like Marianne Faithfull or Frances Farmer. Instead I look like Truman Capote in drag. Oh well, I'm in the right place for that, at least.

✠

It's Wednesday night, early, and I am at home by myself, absolutely without plans and without structure. I sleep until noon, then drag waking and showering out into a multi-hour event. I play at writing, not on the forgotten screenplay but a short story—again, about the Blacklite. I consider going there, under the pretense of doing research, but remember that I have no job, no prospects, and bills to pay. I decide—wisely, I think—to stay in, maybe call Rae-lynn and see how Austin is treating her, maybe eat something. I figure I'll walk down to Mister Kim's and get a newspaper so I'll have something to read while I'm eating—reading and eating, one of the simple pleasures of living alone. Congratulating myself on my self-control, I scrounge around the apartment for cash for my newspaper. I come up with exactly fifty-two pennies, which I roll up in a bandanna and take down to the corner to Mister Kim's.

Placing an *LA Times* on the counter, I begin counting my fifty-two pennies. I sit them in neat stacks of ten on top of the newspaper. Mister Kim is not impressed.

"You know why you no have money?"

"I *have* money. I've got exact change. Look—ten, twenty, thirty, forty . . . "

Mister Kim sticks out his index finger and, one by one, knocks over my tidy stacks of coins.

"This not money. This *pennies.* You know why you no have money?"

I figure I'm going to have to play along if I want my newspaper. "No. Why do I no have money?"

"Because," says Mister Kim, leaning in close like he's telling a big secret. "You and your boyfriend spend *all money* on beer."

"What?" I can't believe him. Mister Kim nods vigorously.

"Yah, yah! You and your boyfriend spend *all money* on beer!"

The nerve of Mister Kim, after all the money I spend here. I snatch up my newspaper and leave in a huff, wondering if I'm mad enough to start walking the extra block to the Adobe Mart.

Back at the apartment, I'm enjoying my single-girl dinner of mac and cheese right out of the pot when I hear the KTLA special bulletin jingle break into the white-noise sitcom I'm not really watching. I figure it's another high-speed chase on the freeway, same shit, different day, and turn, only mildly curious, toward the television. On the screen, I see helicopter footage of a blue sign with the name of my street, Normandie, crossed with another street, Florence, which is a few miles south of Hollywood. The camera then zooms down to the street, where a crowd of people are pulling a man out of a truck and beating him.

This in itself is not that disturbing. It's violent and horrible, sure, but Los Angeles can be a violent and horrible

214

place and things like this happen more often than people like to think. The part that makes me realize that this is no ordinary L.A. gang bang is when the helicopter traffic reporter says, with a touch of panic in his voice, "What we don't understand is where the police are. We've called them a dozen times in the last forty minutes as this has unfolded, and it is becoming pretty clear that they're not responding." The camera pans out from where the man is lying on the ground. Behind him, a liquor store is in the process of being looted. Someone picks up a metal canister and throws it at the man's head. I think he may be dead. There are no police anywhere. It's April 29, 1992, and four L.A. policemen have just been found not guilty of using excessive force on Rodney King. I pick up the phone and call Tommy.

"Yeah. Are you by yourself? Do you think you could come up here?" I check and make sure the hallway is clear, and Tommy comes up. He has no television in his apartment. He sits on the futon and watches the footage.

"Holy shit."

"Yeah."

We watch together for about half an hour. It gets worse. There really isn't anything to say beyond "Holy shit," which is said several more times over the course of the broadcast. It's getting dark outside, and we can hear Tommy's phone ringing, Tina, calling to look for him. Eventually she comes and pounds on my door. We stay quiet until we hear her stripper heels clicking down the hall. After her door closes, Tommy reaches into his pocket and pulls out a ten.

215

"You'd probably better get us some beer." I agree 100 percent. Pocketing the ten and checking the hallway again, I scurry down the stairs and out into the incipient riots to grab all the gusto I can.

Q: *First of all, why did he send you out into the riots instead of going himself, and second of all, was it some sense of denial or fear or something stronger that made you need the beer?*

A: *The "who goes" decision was based on pure logic—if Tina spotted him, he wouldn't be able to come back. And our need for beer was a fear-based one—fear that the looters would get all the beer and there wouldn't be any left for us. Even in the face of violence of historic proportions, we have our priorities.*

Over the next twenty-four hours, things go from bad to worse, at least from my self-centered perspective. A dusk-to-dawn curfew is imposed on the city as the riots creep north toward Hollywood. I brave the smoke and violence to head farther north to one of the few grocery stores that hasn't been looted. In line for over an hour with panicked families stocking up on bread and canned goods, I have a cart full of hard liquor, two boxes of Pop Tarts, and a bag of Twizzlers. The essentials. On the way home, I watch looters stream out of broken-glass storefronts, loaded down with cases of beer, electronics, clothes—anything they can carry. There are no police in this part of town yet; they're busy trying to quell the violence in areas that are already worse off than ours. I am more fascinated than I am scared. I've never seen anything like this before. It feels like a fever dream.

That night, everyone in our building crowds onto the front balcony to watch the flames get closer. Even Tina and I are civil to each other. It's all just a little bit surreal. Mister Kim's is spared. We find out later that the Korean merchants guarded their property from the rooftops with rifles. The 7-Eleven is not spared. We can see smoke billowing up from Hollywood Boulevard; the air is filled with the sound of breaking glass. We're anxious but at the same time eager to see what will happen next and how it will all end. It feels like some bizarre audience-participation performance art piece that we're a part of. When a looter comes tearing across the front yard, being fired on from a car barreling down the sidewalk, we move the party inside and watch the rest of the proceedings on television. Seeing as we're all confined to the building, Tommy can't get away to come visit—but I do find a can of Olde English outside of my door in the morning by way of greeting.

I'm still getting my bearings, not quite back to comprehending what is going on and not really wanting to, when the phone rings. Everyone I know is aware that I have no truck with morning telephone calls. For the first couple of hours after I wake up, it's pretty much tabula rasa with an attitude. Stacey used to hold briefings for houseguests when we stayed at her folks' beach house in the summers: "OK, she's about to come out of her room. Do *not* try to talk to her, do *not* try to touch her, and above all, do *not* tease her about being grouchy." Only after I've had a few

217

cups of coffee and a shower am I able to rid my heart of its hatred for all things human. Someone apparently didn't get the memo, though, because my phone is ringing.

"Hello?" I am ready—nay, *eager*—to cuss someone out. I hope it's an ex-boyfriend, or maybe a telemarketer. Sadly, if it's one, the odds are decent that it's the other as well. It turns out to be neither.

"Hi, Anne, this is Greg Donovan." I start fast-forwarding files in my brain to remember at which dive I gave my number to a Greg Donovan when he adds, "From the MFA program at VCU."

"Ohhhhhh, yeah. Hi."

"How's it going?"

"Um, you know . . . *rioty*."

Q: *By using "rioty" in the opening line of your first-ever conversation with the chair of the creative writing program to which you've applied, were you shooting for*

a) *an incredible show of linguistic chutzpah and creativity by coining a whole new word on the spot like it was nothing special*

b) *the same kind of crap you pulled when you tried to throw your entrance interview at William and Mary? Remember, it didn't work there, either*

or

c) *did you simply, in all good faith, think that was a suitable answer?*

A: *The correct answer is c). It was early. Language eludes me before noon. I honestly thought it was a word.*

Greg Donovan takes "rioty" in stride. He is, after all, a man of letters. "Oh, yeah, that's right! You guys have that riot thing happening out there now. Hey, look—straight to the point. I'm calling to let you know that we got your application, and it was one of about a hundred applications for the creative writing program this year. Our program is very small. We only have eleven slots to fill."

I figure this is going to be the part where he tells me they're looking for more literary writers, writers who write poems about good-hearted homeless people, and essays full of thinky thoughts on Joyce and Woolf. I'm ready to tell him it's no skin off my nose, that I know I'm not MFA material, and he'll thank me for playing and I can go make some coffee. I consider cutting in and telling him I already know and that he doesn't have to sugarcoat it any more, when he comes out of left field with this:

"So, be proud. One of those slots is yours if you want it. Congratulations."

"Dude," I say, because that's all I can say while I let this sink in. "You're *kidding*."

"*Dude*," says the chair of the Creative Writing Department, "I'm not."

"So, I'm in?" I figure there's something here I'm not understanding. There has to be.

"If you want in, you're in. I do have some bad news, though," he begins, and I figure this is where they tell me that I am going to be in the remedial MFA classes, and that I have to make all their bunks and type their papers or something, because there is no way this is true otherwise. "You didn't get a graduate teaching assistantship."

219

"That's too bad," I say insincerely, because if there is anything I totally can't imagine myself doing more than being in graduate school, it's teaching. Imagine, a grubby little lowbrow punk like me, standing up in front of a class full of students like I have something to teach them. Indeed! I'm still trying to figure out if I actually *applied* for a graduate teaching assistantship or if I just checked a random box without realizing it when a hail of gunfire whizzes past the window by my head.

"Hey, I have to get out of the window now," I say apologetically, crouching as close to the ground as the phone cord will let me.

"I understand," Greg says. "Call me when things calm down."

I hang up the phone and combat low-crawl on my belly to the bathtub, which I figure is the safest place in the apartment. I drag a pillow and a blanket off the bed as I slither by. I hurl the pillow and blanket over the side of the tub and climb in after them. Lying in the tub as National Guard helicopters circle overhead through the billowing smoke, I stare at the ceiling and ask myself *now what?* I guess it's over.

Q: *You don't sound exactly thrilled to have gotten into graduate school. Did you ever consider saying no?*

A: *I guess I kind of looked at getting into an MFA program like one would look at being chosen as a sacrificial virgin or being called to a religious order. I was so dumbfounded that they picked me that it never occurred to me that I could say no. I just kept expecting that eventually they'd realize they'd made a clerical error or something* *and they'd call me and apologize, and I'd find another day job and stay in Hollywood. Some days I still think they might call.*

✟

"I say we go for it. The police are busy with the big stuff." Tommy and I are at the Blacklite against the advice of everyone in our building and our own better judgment. We're still under the dusk-to-dawn curfew, but a phone call confirmed that the Blacklite was open—until dusk, anyway. Two doors down from the bar, a mob of looters is using a station wagon and a chain to pull the metal gates off the front of a jewelry store. People are walking, not even running, down Sunset Boulevard carrying televisions, VCRs, and cases of beer. On the way here, we passed the Sam Goody store with its entire front window bashed out, everybody and their mother—literally—climbing out with armloads of CDs. (Don't think I didn't consider acquiring the whole Rolling Stones catalog on CD right then; I hate rebuying the CDs of albums I already bought once on vinyl. Catholic guilt kept me from partaking; with all of my other transgressions, somehow I've never been able to steal. Tommy is trying to convince me that I'm being ridiculous.)

"Look at the other nine commandments. You've broken *all* of them."

"I never killed anybody," I correct him.

"Still. We'll only do stores run by huge corporations, like Sam Goody and Vons. We won't touch the mom-and-pop stores." Tommy is dying to participate in the rioting, which he calls "a holiday for the disenfranchised." I remind him that as a white male with blond hair and blue eyes, his disenfranchised cred is sketchy at best.

"I'm an unemployed drug addict," he says, trying to look pitiful.

"You're unemployed *because* you're a drug addict," I remind him, "and besides, your argument is about as convincing as those idiots with purple dreadlocks and a million piercings who complain about being judged by their looks. You did this to yourself."

"You don't love me," Tommy pouts.

"I love you," Aunt Titty offers, and he blows her a kiss.

"Come on, Anne. There's a Sav-On a block from here."

"A *Sav-On?*" I laugh and shake my head. "What, so we can steal *toilet paper*? Preparation H? Come on." I chuckle to myself at the thought of looting a drugstore. Indeed. I look up and Tommy and Aunt Titty are looking at me like I'm the dumbest thing they've seen.

"OK, who was *just* complaining this morning that she has to buy pills on the street now that her connection left town?"

"I do *not* buy them on the street," I say haughtily. "I buy them at Boardner's." From a Mexican guy named Hector. In the men's room. But not on the street.

"Whatever, little Miss White Gloves. The point is, where do you think those pills come from? It ain't the Easter Bunny."

Duh. I hadn't even thought about drugstores as *drug*-stores. Still, the thought of going into a store through a broken window and climbing out with stuff I didn't pay for is too much for me. Not that I'm scared of getting caught, or hurt, or even getting killed. Consequences aren't my motivation. I don't even know for sure what is. I just can't shake the "no stealing" thing. Call it the last taboo. Next to the last, at least. God knows I've been running low on taboos these last few months.

"Well, I'm going to do it," Tommy announces, and, finding no takers, heads off to conquer the Sav-On alone, a drugstore cowboy without a posse.

"Maybe he'll bring us something," I tell Aunt Titty. (I am blissfully free of all taboos when it comes to things that other people stole, especially if they're drugs.)

"What kind of pills you like, honey?" Aunt Titty rummages in her purse, pulling out a variety of brown prescription bottles and lining them up on the bar. "Luvox . . . Xanax . . . 'Mipramines . . . now that, that's just estrogen, you don't need that." She puts one bottle back in her purse.

"I like Xanax," I say, holding out my hand. She opens the bottle and shakes out a half-dozen pills. I'm fascinated. "Are these all *your* prescriptions?"

"Of course they are. Whose do you think they are?" I can't imagine. I don't tell her that I haven't taken a drug that was actually prescribed to me in years.

"How'd you get so many?"

"How? Look at me!" I look at Aunt Titty. In her orange spandex disco dress and Diana Ross wig, she looks like half the patrons of this bar and every girl at Boardner's . . . utterly and mind-numbingly average. "I'm a forty-eight-year-old transvestite streetwalker. If I don't *need* antidepressants, who does?"

"So you just went to the doctor and told him about your life, and he gave you those?"

"Well, I went to about four doctors. You got insurance, honey?" I nod. My coverage lasts through the summer as part of my severance package. "I tell you what. You go right down here to Kaiser Permanente Hospital . . ." she points toward the hospital, which is only about six blocks from my apartment. "You tell them you want to see a psychiatrist. Not a psychologist! A psychologist can't give you nothing. And you tell them you need something for your nerves." She looks me up and down and frowns. "Tell them you lost your job and your boyfriend's a junkie and you can't sleep at night." I smile, because who knew I wouldn't even have to lie? She smiles back and pats me on the shoulder. "They'll fix you right up."

I had no idea it was going to be that easy.

✝

When Tommy comes back to the building from looting the Sav-On, there's a party in full swing in my one-room apartment. Me, Aunt Titty, and three guys from the Saint Francis Mission are making short work of my liquor supply to the tune of *Exile on Main Street*. Tommy, always my knight in shining track marks, grabs my arm and pulls me out into the hall.

"What the hell is going on in there?"

"I'm not exactly sure." I remember Billy trying to close the bar for at least an hour before Titty and I finally left. We'd taken turns sweet-talking him into one more round about half a dozen times. By then it was well after dusk and we'd had to sneak out the back door with him.

When we got around the corner to where my car was parked, the guys from the mission yelled down to us from their window, but the desk clerk wouldn't let us go up, and, well, the next thing I knew, we were all at my place. Scout's honor.

"They've got to leave."

"You're not kidding." One of the guys from the mission really stinks. "Hey, how was the looting?"

"Ahh, it was lame. Everything was already gone. Oh, I got you something." He pulls a tube of Preparation H out of his pocket.

"Smart-ass. Hey, help me get these guys out of here."

"Well, we can't just put them on the street, it's after curfew, and besides, in case you forgot, there's a riot going on. What do you want to do?"

I shrug. "I guess we take 'em back where we got 'em."

Ten minutes later, me, Tommy, Aunt Titty, and the homeless guys are creeping through the deserted streets of Hollywood in my Hyundai with the headlights off. There is no one, absolutely no one, on the streets of Los Angeles. I feel like I am in a low-budget science fiction movie where the aliens have come down and scooped up everyone but a handful (or a Hyundai-full) of junkies, drag queens, and hoboes. I've never seen Los Angeles like this.

Apparently, tonight is the night for a lot of people to see things they've never seen before. The baby-faced National Guard soldier who pulls us over doesn't know what to make of this particular bunch of curfew breakers.

"Turn on the tears, baby," Aunt Titty mutters to me as the soldier walks toward the driver's window. If I wasn't planning to cry, the rifle pointed at my face works as an excellent motivator.

"Good evening, folks." He shines the light on me, then Tommy, then across the back seat, stopping on Aunt Titty long enough for her to manage a crocodile tear or two herself. "Are you all aware there's a curfew for the city in effect?"

"That's why," I say, trying my best to tear up, "we were tryin' to get *home*!" In addition to the tears, I turn on the southern accent. I figure if it works on cops it might work on soldiers, too.

"Well, are you *close*?" He looks perplexed, like he'd rather deal with gangbangers or something else they'd actually briefed him for before they put him on this corner.

I nod vigorously and dab at my eyes. "Uh huh, yes, sir," I sob, feeling utterly ridiculous calling an eighteen-year-old kid "sir" but hoping he'll be flattered enough to let me go.

"I want you to listen to me very carefully," he says wearily, shining his flashlight across the back seat one more time. "I want you to go straight home, do not stop anywhere, and I want you to *stay there*. And if I see you again tonight . . ." he shines the flashlight in my face for emphasis. "I'm going to arrest you. You got that?"

"Yes, sir. Thank you, sir. I promise, sir!"

"Thank you, baby!" cries Aunt Titty, giving him a Miss America wave, and I peel out, leaving the poor guardsman looking like he might cry, too. They prepare you for a lot of things in the military, but I'll bet they didn't prepare him for us.

Q: *So did you turn around and go straight home?*

A: *Are you kidding? I only* look *honest. There was no way I was bringing those guys back to my place again. We completed the mission and then went straight home. Scout's honor.*

✠

Less than a week after the end of the riots, I show up at Kaiser Permanente for the appointment that I hope will be my ticket to legitimate pharmaceutical relief. I am actually on time for my appointment, so eager am I to avail myself of white-market pharmaceuticals at co-pay prices. I'm wearing my most subdued interview clothes—a black skirt, business pumps, and a tan silk jacket—on Aunt Titty's advice, trying my hardest to look like a nice little girl who's just under too much stress.

"Hi, my name is Anne Soffee and I have a two o'clock appointment to see a psychiatrist."

The receptionist looks up and down her page, then flips forward a page, then back a page. She taps the calendar with her pencil.

"Honey, your appointment was *yesterday*." Shit! This unemployment crap has me all mixed up. I never know what day it is any more. "That's OK, just have a seat," she says, scratching out my name and flipping through the book some more. "I'm sure somebody can see you. I'll see who we have with a slot available."

I sit down, relieved that I'm not going to have to get up at the crack of lunch again tomorrow. After a while, a tiny woman with a shock of white-blonde hair and over-sized orange spectacles motions for me to come back to her office. I go in and sit down and she introduces herself as Carole, staff psychologist.

"Oh, well, there's been a mistake," I say, getting up to leave. "I'm supposed to see a psychiatrist. That's what I requested." She motions for me to sit back down.

"Everyone has to see the psychologist first," she says. "That's how we determine what you need." Drat. I try and remember the coaching Aunt Titty has given me, the things I'm supposed to say and not say. If what I remember is correct, the worse my life is, the more likely I am to get lots and lots of prescriptions, but I'm not to mention any drugs specifically or let on that I've been taking anything up until now. Carole gets out a clipboard and starts asking me questions, starting with the basics and then getting more abstract. "So what brings you to us? Why do you think you need help?"

"Well, I'm under a lot of stress." Good start. I take a breath and start counting off stressors on my fingers. "I got laid off from my job—oh, and right before that happened, my best friend, well, my only friend really, she moved to Texas. And I don't really have anyone to talk to about it, you know, because my family is *really* far away. Oh, except my boyfriend. Only he's a heroin addict. And I can't really talk to him that much anyway, because he has another girlfriend so we can't see each other so often because we have to sneak."

"Really." She makes some notes. She doesn't seem the least bit impressed by my story, which worries me.

"Oh, and my boyfriend's girlfriend lives two apartments down from me." Carole raises an eyebrow and makes
a note. "It's *very* stressful," I add.

"Yes, it sounds like it could be," she says. She makes
some more notes on the clipboard then looks through some
papers on her desk.

"It sounds like the best fit for you would be our codependency education program. Do you know anything about
codependency?"

I know that it sounds like another hot California buzz-
word but I don't let on. I shake my head.

"Well, simply put, it's a dysfunctional relationship
pattern. It means that your self-esteem is tied into an
enabling relationship, usually with an alcoholic or an
addict."

If I had a cookie, I would give it to her for using
that many therapeutic buzzwords in one sentence. In any
case, it sure doesn't sound like a ticket to prescription
relief. I frown.

"I don't think that's my thing. What else have you got?"

Carole looks perplexed. She puts down her clipboard
and folds her hands. "I'll tell you what," she says, leaning
back in her chair. Her tiny frame is lost in the huge leather
chair. She looks like Edith Ann. "I want you to come back
and see me once a week. We'll talk about some options for
you and see what else we can work out."

"I don't have all the time in the world," I say. "I'm
moving back to Virginia in July, so I only have a couple of
months." Unspoken message: *Hand over the scrips, lady, and
stop wasting my time.*

Carole is nonplussed. "We don't need all the time in the world," she says blithely. "We'll just take it one day at a time."

GAH! I hightail it out of her office and back to the Blacklite, to talk to Aunt Titty about what went wrong.

✠

Titty tells me that the best I can do is go back to Carole and try again. I go back, twice, without the first prescription being written or even mentioned as a possible solution. Titty tells me to kick it up a little, really give her some stories from my horribly stressful life.

"Tell her about that night that that asshole punched Tommy in the nose for hitting him with a dart!" I only vaguely remember that night. I was in the bathroom when the actual fight happened. When I came out, the puncher had been thrown out the door so hard he'd broken his wrist on the pavement. I felt sorry for him and drove him to the hospital, then I cussed out the nurse when she said he'd have to make a statement about how it happened, which he'd already told me he wasn't about to do because he had a habeas out on him. She called the police and we had to make a break for it, the poor guy holding his wrist and howling in pain.

"OK, what else?"

"Tell her about the time that suit came in here and said you weren't a lady." That was some night, too. I was standing at the jukebox, drinking a bottle of Budweiser, and some business Joe who obviously didn't know from the Blacklite walked up and tried to talk to me. Billy asked if he wanted to "buy the lady a drink" and he said that if I was a lady I'd be drinking from a glass, not the bottle.

The nerve! Billy got out the biggest mug in the place, filled it with beer, and handed it to Brandi. She walked up to the suit and just as sweet as you please batted her eyes and asked, "Am *I* a lady?" Then, without waiting for an answer, she dumped it over his head.

"But those stories don't even have anything to do with me, really," I worry.

"Yes, but they're good stories," Aunt Titty says, and I guess they are. I worry that there is too much alcohol in both of them, though. Over the past couple of sessions, Carole has been pushing me less toward the codependency program and more toward the substance abuse one. She's a nice lady, and I know she means well, but I can't figure out how she is so off-base on this one. I can't make her see that Tommy is the one with the drug problem and I'm the one with the stress problem. It doesn't occur to me that I probably reek of alcohol every time she sees me and that every stressful incident I relay in our sessions takes place in a bar.

"I want you not to drink between now and our next meeting," says Carole. "Do you think you can do that?" Can I? Of *course* I can. Will I? That's another story.

"*Ginger ale?*" says Billy indignantly. He looks like I've hurt his feelings. "What's with that?"

"I just have a lot of stuff to do tonight," I say.

"No, you don't." He knows me too well. He puts a ginger ale and a shot of Jack Daniels in front of me. I get all misty; Jack and ginger is what Keith Richards drinks. It's what Stacey and I used to drink on his birthday every year. I pour the shot into the ginger ale and play "Brown Sugar" on the jukebox. *I'll quit tomorrow,* I tell myself, and Billy winks at me.

epilogue

Tattoo Me
What the World Needs Now Is Olallaberry Pie

i could devote a whole book to all of the humiliating
and deeply personal details that finally allow me to
consider that Carole might have a point. You could
then file this book between Elizabeth Wurtzel and Who the
Fuck Cares on the sad-little-overeducated-girls-with-sub-
stance-abuse-problems shelf. This ain't that kind of party,
and besides, I'd like to maintain a shred of human dignity,
or at least be able to pretend that I have.

After a particularly demoralizing weekend, Carole
finally convinces me to take in an AA meeting—"Just to
see what it's like, no commitments, no strings." She and I
look over a schedule and decide that the ten o'clock "late
night" meeting at the Hollywood Recovery Center would
be the best choice for me. I get the feeling that she's deliberately screwing up my drinking schedule, but what the
hey. I've grown to trust Carole more than I ever thought
I would at that first session just two weeks ago. We've
covered a lot of ground in a little time; since I am scheduled
to leave Los Angeles in forty-five days, Carole has me coming in almost daily. She gained big points with me in our
most recent session when she told me that she used to be
the resident ditzy blonde on the Wolfman Jack show. Her
job was to giggle a lot and say "I don't know, Wolfman!"

whenever he asked a question. I figure if anybody can pull my butt out of the tailspin it's been in for the past year, Wolfman Jack's bimbo sidekick can. (I may not have met my goal of becoming the next Lester Bangs, but even in feel-good California therapy, I go for the rock 'n' roll irony.)

At nine o'clock that night I set out to walk to the Hollywood Recovery Center. Hollywood Boulevard is just starting to come alive. I do my best to fade into the dingy brick of the tourist shops and dive bars in my tank top, overalls, and sloppy ponytail. It's been weeks since I've bothered to drag up before going out to the bars; why would I bother to drag up for a meeting? In spite of my ragged appearance, a number of the cars that drive past slow down, check me out, and make offers. *Hey mamacita . . . you working?* Am I working? What do they take me for, I wonder—the world's laziest hooker? I walk on, ignoring the offers and thinking about what I may or may not give up.

I've told Carole again and again that I'm not ready for the concept of life *without*. I tell her I need the option of taking a Xanax or a Valium when Tommy chooses Tina over me, and I need to be able to relax with a beer when I get all knotted up over how long I'll be able to pull off the graduate school facade before they realize they've made a horrible mistake. Those are the bad times, when I *need* something. Then there are the *good* times, when I *want* something. Last night was Billy's birthday, and we celebrated and toasted all night long. I brought him a rose made out of red wrapper Trojans and a card that said "I would have gotten you something cheap, but you already have me." Brandi dressed up in a cowgirl outfit with assless chaps and a G-string. We went into the ladies' room and I wrote "Happy Birthday Billy" across her cheeks and stuck the rose in between. She sashayed out of the bathroom and bent over the jukebox casually, like she was looking for a song, and the whole bar went wild. I can't imagine never having any more nights like that. How do normal people stand it?

"Cheer up, honey." I look up and see a dark-haired girl, a real streetwalker, in jeans and a halter top, leaning on a pair of crutches. "It ain't that bad." I take it as a sign, as anyone probably should when the crippled hookers start giving them sympathetic advice.

I can hear a motorcyclist cruising slowly behind me, and I pick up my pace. I keep my head down, eyes passing over the grime-encrusted stars on Hollywood Boulevard. Imogene Coca, Eartha Kitt, Montgomery Clift. Hollywood might have let me down, but at least I'm not the only one. I imagine all of the Midwestern families who come on vacation, expecting glamour and gloss. Hollywood today is washed-up metal bands and crippled hookers—and one very nervous southern girl on her way to a late-night meeting. The motorcyclist revs his engine and speeds ahead.

Two blocks later, he is back, idling in the crosswalk, blocking my path. I have to look up to cross the street, and when I do, I meet his eyes. *Travis Bickle,* I think. He looks like De Niro. A dashing psychopath on a purple-flake Harley. He revs the motor, twisting with a tattooed hand. I look away but I can still feel him staring at me. I figure he must be wondering what turnip truck I fell off. In a few weeks, I'll be back in Virginia, buying school supplies and seeing if I can get my old job back at the mall. *It will be just like I never left,* I think dejectedly. *Three years in Los Angeles and nothing to show for it.*

At the next intersection, the motorcycle is parked on the curb, silent. Travis Bickle is leaning back on the leather seat, arms crossed, feet on the handlebars. I move to walk around the bike and he swings his feet down, boots hitting the pavement with a thud.

"What'sa matter?" His New York accent is thick and taunting. "You can't stop and say hi?"

"Hi," I say, and try to walk around the bike.

"Where ya goin' in such a hurry?"

"That's some more of your business," I say, trying to sound tough.

He looks me up and down and nods. "You must be goin' to a meeting."

I am confused, impressed, and maybe a little offended. Surely there are other places on Hollywood Boulevard that people go at night; how many times have I walked down this same street to go to bars, the newsstand, or just to the *taqueria* for some dinner? Is it that obvious? Am I the last one to see the giant arrow pointing at my head? He grins and nods when I don't respond. He's found me out.

"Check this out," he says, dropping his leather jacket onto the seat of the bike. He pulls off his black T-shirt, too, revealing muscled arms completely sleeved with inkwork, a chained heart with a banner that reads "Carla" over one pierced nipple, and, when he turns his back to me, huge Olde English letters across his shoulders that read "LIVING SOBER."

He picks up his shirt and puts it back on. Then he gets on the bike, throws me the jacket, and motions to the seat behind him. "Get on," he says.

And I do.

✠

We pull up in front of a one-story bungalow off Melrose Avenue. *This isn't the Hollywood Recovery Center,* I think to myself as Travis Bickle parks the bike and helps me off. *I guess now is when he buries me under the porch.*

"The meeting is at ten," I say hopefully.

"That meeting is full of pussies and crybabies," he says. "You didn't want to go to that one." He unlocks the front door and we walk into an empty living room. There is no furniture and the walls are stark white. Peering down a hallway, I see another white room, this one with a king-sized mattress on the floor.

"Do you live here?" All signs are pointing to serial killer at this point, but I feel a lot like I did at the Iggy Pop concert—at least it's a memorable way to go.

"I don't like no clutter," he says, leading me into the kitchen. In the middle of the kitchen sits an antique dentist's chair. I am intrigued. I walk around it.

"I tattoo," he says proudly. "Little hobby. You want a tattoo? That's a good first date thing, huh? A tattoo?"

I look at him to see if he is serious. He appears to be. The fact that I don't refuse immediately seems to encourage him. He grabs a photo album from the counter.

"Look at my stuff. I'm good," he says, flipping through the pages. "I don't do nothin' free, either. You're getting star treatment, a free tattoo from Danny. It's 'cos it's a date, that's why."

I look at the pictures. They look good, but what do I know from tattoos? A tattoo is something I have always sort of wanted, but a tattoo is not really a *sort* of thing. It occurs to me that this might not even be his portfolio, that getting me in the chair could be the prelude to hacking me into little bits. So I ask a very reasonable question.

"Can you do a Danzig logo on my stomach?"

"Danzig? That guy's a little *weenie*."

"How about a Rolling Stones one, on my shoulder?"

"This stuff you want, this rock 'n' roll stuff, that's fuckin' crap," he says impatiently. "Lemme show you what I want to do. Get in the chair."

I am taken aback. This is getting a little too real. I ask if I can call Tommy and see what he thinks. Travis Bickle pounds a fist on the counter and yells "You gotta call somebody else and ask them about something that's gonna be on *your* body for the rest of your life?" He runs a hand through his greasy hair. "What'sa matter? You can't think for yourself?" He points again to the chair. "Get in the chair!"

And I do.

✝

To say that Carole is disappointed with the way my evening turned out is an understatement. I spend my entire next session convincing her that I don't need a weeklong inpatient detox to save me from myself. It does not impress her in the least that I haven't had a drink since our last session.

It also doesn't impress her that I've hardly been seeing Tommy at all; of course, that's not entirely been my choice, as Tina has been doing her best Dragon Lady impression since the riots. With everyone confined to the two-story building from dusk until dawn for the duration of the curfew, Tommy and I did an exceptionally poor job of hiding our liaisons from the rest of the tenants, and hell hath no fury like an aging strip-o-gram dancer scorned.

Carole stammers a lot about choices and patterns and boundary issues, all the while pushing for me to commit to round-the-clock supervision until I leave L.A. I finally agree to a compromise—an intensive outpatient program and a contract to go to a meeting every night. I don't have a problem with the outpatient program; it's a lot like school. I take notes, do worksheets, and raise my hand a lot. That I can do. It's the meetings that I'm not too sure about, but I promise to give it a shot.

Q: *You're fudging again. What about the tattoo?*

A: *Right, the tattoo. It's an abstract scorpion in red and black Maori style. A combination of two of the cheesiest aspects of tattooing—astrological signs and phony tribal designs. On my chest, which, after the ankle and the completely unoriginal small of the back, is the cheesiest spot for a girl to have a tattoo. The sad thing is it's not quite cheesy enough to be ironic; it's just . . . cheesy.*

I decide to try the pussies and crybabies meeting again, this time taking a circuitous route to avoid running into Travis Bickle. I'm actually worried that he might be at the meeting itself, but he's not. He would fit right in if he were; the meeting is about one-third bikers, one-third rockers, and one-third unknown quantities like me. I help myself to a Styrofoam cup full of bad instant coffee and sit down next to a bear of a guy with a gray beard and wire-rimmed glasses. People take turns talking about their stressful lives—breakups and layoffs, bill collectors and child support. Grand jury indictments. Each story is more miserable than the last, it seems to me, but after each tale of woe, the speaker cheerfully adds a qualifier along the lines of " . . . and I choose not to drink over that." The idea!

The bearded man seated next to me speaks toward the end of the meeting. His name is Fisher, and he identifies himself as "an addict, alcoholic, nerd, and geek." Dude. I'm so there. He shares about feeling like he's not as cool as everyone else in this meeting but that he earned his seat just like they did. Nods all around. After Fisher, a guy who looks like Mickey Rourke also identifies as an addict, alcoholic, nerd, and geek. I don't speak up, but inside I'm thinking *that's me, too.*

After the meeting, Fisher shakes my hand and asks if I need a lift home. He has three guys in tow, his sponsees, he calls them, who look like the bastard love children of Keith Richards and Johnny Thunders. If Carole could see me now, she'd yank me out by my ear, but she needn't worry because my head is so busy digesting the concept of addict, alcoholic, nerd, and geek that I'm not even thinking in that direction. We pile into Fisher's rust bucket Datsun and putter off toward my apartment in a cloud of highly California-illegal gray exhaust.

As we smokescreen our way down Hollywood Boulevard, I continue to mull my future as an alcoholic nerd. So engrossed am I in the speculation, that when one of the sponsees gestures out the window and snickers, "Check it out, there goes C. C. DeVille," I don't even look up. (I'm sorry, Stacey. I owe you one. I just had a lot on my mind.) Within blocks, my reverie is interrupted by Fisher rapping on the dash with a sparkly lucite baton.

"Hit it, guys," says Fisher, and I squirm around in my seat to see what they're going to hit. In the back seat, the Keithlets grab big plastic dinosaurs out of the rear windshield and wave them slowly side to side.

"What the world needs now . . . is love, sweet love . . ." The Keithlets croak in unison, wagging the dinosaurs at passing cars. I'm fascinated, partly by what this has to do with anything and partly because I never met any guys who looked as cool as these guys but were willing to make such idiots of themselves with total abandon. None of the guys at Boardner's would be caught dead singing Dionne Warwick songs and waving plastic dinosaurs, much less in a Datsun. They keep singing, and I turn and look at Fisher for explanation.

"It's the only song the brontosaurus knows," Fisher explains. "We're going to the House of Pies; olallaberries are in season. Wanna come?"

"No, thanks," I say, figuring I already have a lot to digest without pie.

"Well, maybe next time. You coming tomorrow?"

"I don't know." Right now I am thinking yes, but it's still daunting, this whole *without* thing. It's a long time from now until ten o'clock tomorrow night, and between now and then there's Tommy, and Mister Kim, and the Blacklite if I end up needing a drink between now and then, I probably won't feel like coming back. What would be the point?

"It's the only thing that there's just too little of . . ."

"This is my building, here." The Datsun putters to a stop in the middle of the street. As I gather up my pamphlets and fliers, Tina comes out of the building in her sexy nurse strip-o-gram outfit.

"Hellllooooooooo, nurse," howl the Keithlets.

"I *like* your building," says Fisher, watching her arrange her stethoscope in her cleavage.

I look up on the balcony and see Tommy leaning against the railing. A red and gold tallboy rests on the table beside him and a cigarette dangles from his lips. He points at Tina, walking down the street toward her car, then motions for me to hurry up and come inside.

"On second thought," I say to Fisher, "if it's not too late, I think I would like some pie."

"Pie it is," he says, checking his rearview mirror and making an illegal U-turn in the middle of Normandie Avenue. "From the top, boys!"

"What the world needs now . . . is love, sweet love . . ."
Over the dinosaur chorus, I hear the clattering of a red and gold tallboy can hitting the street behind our car. Looking back, I can see the streetlight illuminating it as it rolls toward the gutter, glinting gold. I turn around and close my eyes, listening to the dinosaurs sing.

Also by Anne Thomas Soffee

Snake Hips

*Belly Dancing and
How I Found True Love*

"Hilarious."
— *New York Times*

"Toss the Prozac and grab a tambourine—
I very much like Soffee's idea that a woman can belly dance
her way out of heartache."
— Tom Robbins, author of *Even Cowgirls Get the Blues*

"Full of belly laughs."
— *People*

"Her prose sparkles and teases."
— *Boston Globe*

"Told with honesty, humility, and hilarity."
— *USA Today*

"*Snake Hips* is a hip, funny, and uplifting memoir . . . the
perfect pick-me-up for the newly single."
— *Grace* magazine

"A vigorous, funny account of the effects of a blighted
romance cured, sort of, by a course in belly dancing."
— *Kirkus*

"Soffee's witty, flowing prose draws readers in."
— *Booklist*

"Lively, wry book."
— *Chicago Sun-Times*

**CHICAGO
REVIEW
PRESS**

Paper, $14.95 (CAN $22.95)
5½ x 8½, 155652-522-2

Distributed by Independent Publishers Group
www.ipgbook.com

Available at your local bookstore, or call (**800**) **888-4741**.